THE CLASS OF COVID-19

Deluxe Edition:
Volumes I and II

Cliffside Park High School

THE CLASS OF COVID-19

Deluxe Edition:
Volumes I and II

In memory of grandmas and grandpas, moms and dads, coaches, proms, graduations, friends, holidays, dreams, and other lost things.

"The inferno of the living is not something that will be; if there is one, it is what is already here, the inferno where we live every day, that we form by being together. There are two ways to escape suffering it. The first is easy for many: accept the inferno and become such a part of it that you can no longer see it. The second is risky and demands constant vigilance and apprehension: seek and learn to recognize who and what, in the midst of inferno, are not inferno, then make them endure, give them space." —*Italo Calvino, Invisible Cities*

CONTENTS

VOLUME II
Second Wave

141

Preface

This opportunity to read about stories and then comment on their meaning, significance, and honesty is truly breathtaking. Really. These students at Cliffside Park High School are heroes themselves in facing down COVID-19, the pandemic which has brought hell to Americans and many around the world. These stories you are about to read in this book are going to help us face the pandemic. They are not third-party narratives but rather in-person perceptions of families, relatives, friends etc. These are the dreams and nightmares of young adults struggling with a cruel virus. Each story is a deeply felt experience.

As I write the preface, I understand my responsibilities as a public official, but I am most conscious of these young writers trying to grapple with the Second Wave of sickness and death and the emotional isolation which accompanies. Simply put, our Cliffside Park talented students show us all their deeply felt humanity beyond the selfishness of our modern age. Thanks to all of you for helping elevate the discussion of our present condition.

I want to hug you all.

Congressman Bill Pascrell,
U.S. Representative for N.J.

Introduction to the Deluxe Edition

In my mid-thirties, when I decided to leave the world of retail and become an educator, I was fortunate enough to have a mentor named John Browne, who was assigned to supervise my student teaching. One time while he was watching, a student asked me a hard question. "I don't know," I said. "I'll have to get back to you." He was impressed by that and made sure to validate me afterwards. "The bravest thing we can do as educators, the most beneficial and important," he said, "is to admit that we don't always have all the answers."

The first edition of this book came out in June and included forty-nine student stories. Fears at that time were acute as our area was hard hit. Students had tangible losses and immediate concerns. I remember vividly that on the day I announced to the class we were going to write a book of our stories, I took a walk near a local nursing home. They had so many people die so quickly, they were throwing bodies into a mobile refrigeration unit.

As a result, the stories in the first edition were mostly about concrete things. We called them "lost things:" proms and graduations and people. Re-reading these stories now, I am impressed by their variety and specificity.

Because of this, in the introduction to that book I talked about dreams. "Thank you for sharing my students' dreams with them," I wrote. I thought this could be an affirmational, redemptive salve against a generational sickness.

But if the first edition was about dreams, the second edition is full of waking nightmares. Students talk of the never-ending roller coaster due to COVID and a world without God and how everything seems fake. They write of repetition and the existential horrors of feeling both unsafe and without hope. As I write this introduction, our country has more daily cases and more daily deaths and more daily hospitalizations than ever.

It's not even Thanksgiving yet. Winter is coming.

I admit now I do not know. I do not know why some people live and some people die. I do not know why most adults have failed us on every level. I do not know if there can be heroes or redemption during a plague. I do not know why bad things happen to good people. I do not know why I am here for all my faults and sins and others are not. I do not know why the country is sick and the people are sick and we are sick. I do not know how to let go of lost things, and I do not know how any of this will get better. I don't even really know if I ever got COVID.

What I do know is that the only chance we have to figure any of this out is to figure it out by listening to the stories of our most vulnerable, by amplifying their voices, by supporting their sharing, and by giving them power. I am so lucky to have gotten a chance to know these kids – to hear them, to work with them, to laugh with them and cry with them. I'm certain each and every one of them is going to change the world. That is my dream.

Thank you for sharing my dream with me.

—Shawn Adler (November 2020)

Benjamin Luderer

My name is Ben Luderer, and I am currently a senior. I have been blessed with great parents who have been able to give me many special opportunities throughout my life. These opportunities range from private drum lessons to flying around the country for athletic events.

I spent much of my childhood participating in seasonal activities. During the fall and the winter, my parents and I were wrapped up in the wonderful world of youth ice hockey. In the spring, I was involved in baseball. As for the summer, I attended a variety of different day camps and sleep away camps. I also traveled with my family, taking trips to numerous states and foreign countries including Canada, France, and Great Britain.

With all the activities I participated in, it is hard to believe I had time for my education. Through eighth grade, I was a student in the River Vale Public School system. In elementary school, I participated in all the town sports as well as most of the school sponsored activities. When I was in middle school, I was the first sixth grader to make the middle school baseball team which was the first step in my focus on baseball.

During eighth grade, I took trips to visit different catholic schools with my best friend, even though at the time I had no intention of attending any of them. When I visited Don Bosco Prep, I immediately fell in love with the school. Being public school teachers, both of my parents strongly believe in the public-school system. It took some convincing for them to agree to a non-public school. They now admit that Don Bosco turned out to be the best place for me academically, socially, and athletically. I wound up being a four-year letter winner for baseball, making the All-State team in my senior year and earning several scholarships to Division One schools. Although I was offered the chance to play baseball professionally out of high school, I chose instead to go to college.

I began my career at Marist College as a biomedical science major but changed to Psychology/Special Education after the summer of my freshman year. During the summer of my freshman year, I lived in upstate New York to play baseball. There, I spent off-days working with children in schools, and I loved it. Becoming a teacher has always been an option in my mind, mostly because I saw the life my parents lived, and the type of life they were able to give me.

Ultimately, I would like to be a school psychologist, but I feel to be a successful or effective psychologist I would benefit from classroom experience interacting with students. I look forward to the experience I will gain through my student teaching placement.

Editor's Note: Ben Luderer, who wrote this memoir when he was in college, died of complications from the Coronavirus on March 30, 2020. He was 30. He achieved his goal and became a teacher and a coach at Cliffside Park High School. He was beloved.

VOLUME I

Insights from the Inside

One

By Ariana Castillo

I always wanted to be part of history. Who wouldn't want to witness something that would be talked about for years to come? It's been my dream for the longest to live through something extraordinary. I no longer have any desire whatsoever to be part of history. I just want normal.

I don't think I have ever missed having a normal school day like I do now. For the past month, I have been in quarantine and been confined to my house. I've only left for quick anxiety-filled trips to the grocery store for essentials. There's a pandemic that basically took over the world without any warning and changed everything. The "Invisible Enemy" is what the government calls it. Every aspect of what I used to consider my boring life changed in what felt like the snap of a finger. My boring, normal life. I don't think I have ever appreciated that life until a few weeks ago. When

I first heard about COVID-19, I thought that it was just another over-exaggerated event that would be over in weeks, if not days.

At least that's what my teachers told me. That's what my parents believed. Even my boss at my job repeated that this was just a precaution, a big over-exaggerated response. I believed this. This was normal. More so, I didn't care about it. If someone would have told me right then and there "hey, this is going to go down in history forever," I probably would have laughed in their face. What history? The one I had studied all my life? I didn't believe future generations would be studying what was happening to people like me who lived through this: this pandemic. I was much more worried about choosing the university I would be attending in just a few months. I cared more about figuring out which house would suit my friends and I the best for our prom weekend. I stressed more about where to buy my overpriced dress that I was going to wear once at prom.

I didn't have time to even get a full night's sleep, because I was too busy with my life and dealing with these last few months of high school. I didn't care about some virus that was going on in Europe. I lived in America. I lived ten minutes from the biggest city in the world. A virus that no one took seriously here was none of my concern. I could see my friends. I could plan my future. But I guess that's what happens now, when you live through history. Life changes while you are living through history.

I always knew how dramatic events such as pandemics and wars had happened in the blink of an eye. I studied it, and I loved learning every second of this history, and how it shaped the world I live in now. You'd think someone who studied such history would have realized when they themselves were forming part of a new one. I remember reading about how lives were changed forever during events like these, and how easy it was for everyday normal routines to be shattered. I used to think that was a bit exaggerated to be honest.

History is often weird like this and complex. Only reading about what happened doesn't always give us a full account of what truly went on. I believe now that we need to live through something to fully understand it. Events like these aren't over in months like government officials will tell you, or just because we want it to be, or even because we have advanced technology. This was the same story that was told on numerous occasions to people over time when things like this happened.

This is the same story we were being told right now. I am living through history, and acting just like the people I read about in my history classes. There's a weight of that story now for me - a feeling of uncertainty that wasn't there before. I feel the colossal doubt, the loss of hope, the sadness, and the general grief for every little thing that changes daily in my life. Every aspect of what once thought could never be taken away, or be changed, has been. The normal we take for granted. We don't see it until we are living it, until it is gone and we become the people who have to deal with it.

This is it now. This is history. These are the stories. This is the new normal.

Two

By Christian Cruz

The ducks swimming in the stream caught my attention immediately as I made my way to my sister and dad. I followed them as they rode their bikes towards a nice view by the stream. My sister, Emily, wanted to take a picture by the stream with the ducks. As she struggled to pose for the picture, a large gust of wind blew behind her, and soon enough her once-perfect hair was in a jumbled mess on her face. I took a seat on a large rock near the edge of the stream and watched. Behind us my mom followed close, making sure my brother didn't fall off of his scooter. My dad couldn't resist laughing as she tried to fix her hair to no avail. My mom joined in on the laughter, while my dad tried to console Emily for her now wasted hour of curling her hair in the morning.

My family was on the other side of the park by now, near a bridge over the stream. My mom and sister posed, as my dad snapped a picture of them embracing on the bridge. I watched from afar, appreciating the calmness in the air which I had not felt in a long time. I watched the ducks wading on the stream for another moment, glad everything was under control.

My dad was one month sober on that day.

I woke up one morning feeling lazy and upset that the sun was shining brightly exactly on the side of the bed where I lay. It was exactly one month since quarantine began, and I was only getting lazier by the day. It was still early, and I decided to go back to sleep until 8:00 am, but a rustling downstairs caught my attention. I sat up in a slight panic, as I tried to figure out what was going on. Today was the first day of my mom's new shift at work. I made my way out of my room to wish her goodbye when I saw my dad with her. They were on the way out. He was dropping her off.

"Good morning, mijo" my mom said.

I could tell my dad was in a hurry to leave.

"Good morning" I said, somewhat confused.

"Do you want to come drop me off with your dad?"

I had just woken up and was not ready to go out. I wanted to say no, but I knew I couldn't. To my surprise, my dad spoke before me.

"It's okay, we're already running late and he's not ready"

My mom and I looked at each other with concern and asked him if he was sure. I noticed he was holding the drone my sister and I gifted him for Christmas.

"What's the drone for? You sure you don't want me to go with you?" I asked.

"I'm just taking it to fly it outside by mom's work, so it's alright don't worry."

I recognized that something wasn't right. He had not left the house without someone by his side for almost two months. Yet I trusted him. Before I could say anything else, my dad was already out the door, and my mom followed behind. She wished me good-bye, and they were gone.

The familiar anxiety which I had felt for the past year returned that day. As I finished online classes, my dad had still not returned. My texts were left unanswered. My calls went to voicemail. My mind raced. There were a million places he could be, and I feared one place most of all. The fact that I did not insist on going with him in the morning made my stomach bitter. My anxiety skyrocketed as I tried to figure out what to do and where he could be.

Then he called me.

"I'm going to wait by your mom's work until it's her lunch time, that way I can eat with her. Do you guys need anything at home? Your mom asked me to buy her food and to bring it to her. If you want, I could drop off some food for you guys at home too."

I had made and packed my mom's lunch the night before. I saw her leave the house with her lunch that morning. In the midst of my panic, I was quiet on the phone.

"What is it?" he asked.

I couldn't think of anything to say.

I finally replied, "Are you sure you don't want to pick me up so I can go along with you?"

"No, it's alright" was all he said.

Later that night, he left home by himself again. All I could think about was why I didn't go with him that morning.

"Let's pray"

My mom looked at me with surprise in her eyes. This was the first time I had ever suggested that we pray.

We had been sitting on the living room couch for an hour, anxious and worried. My dad had just stormed out of the house. After an hour spent arguing about why he shouldn't go out on his own, and after pleading with him to follow the 8:00 pm curfew he swore by just two weeks ago - we lost. After spending a week worrying about where he was going every night, my mother and I had come to the conclusion that my father relapsed. We could tell by the look of desperation and detachment in his face that the father we knew wasn't present anymore. His dilated pupils told us the whole story. There was nothing my mom and I could do.

"The hardest part about dealing with addiction is accepting we are not in control," I told her.

That was a phrase which I had heard a thousand times already from talking heads discussing COVID and the pandemic, yet that was the first time I understood it. That night we prayed, asking for my father to return, and for God to give my father the strength he desperately needed. That night, alone and inside after many weeks of quarantine, I dreamt about more days in the park.

Three

By Christian Osuna

I walked through the open door and saw my mother holding her very last check; I knew it would be a long time before I saw her holding another. My mother's final check made me realize that there would be no more ordering out, shopping for new clothes, or going out. I also knew that soon I would no longer be working at the restaurant where I was making a good amount of money for someone my age. I knew my mother was worried about the pandemic, but I think her biggest concern was the rent and the other bills that would eventually pile up if we both did not return to work. I wanted to remain hopeful that this would eventually blow over and that my mother and I would be able to go back to work, but that seemed highly unlikely. I started to consider applying for a job as a delivery driver or working in construction. My mother did not qualify for any type of aid. I was torn with the difficult decision to ask my father for help.

My mother and father were deeply in love but their relationship came to an end when my father was not brave enough to stand up to his family. My mother never asked my father for a single penny and she chose to raise me without his help. However, now we needed all the help we could get. I knew my mother would not have approved of asking for money, but I felt that I had no other choice. I did not want my mother to stress over paying the bills when my father had made enough income from his successful business in another country. Every time we spoke on the phone, my father would always tell me that if I ever needed anything to not hesitate and ask. So when my father and I spoke on the phone to catch up, I took the call as an opportunity to tell him what my mother and I were going through. My father immediately wired money into my bank account.

My father told me he would send money weekly to ensure my mother and I were more than comfortable. The amount my father was sending for the week was more than enough to cover living expenses for the entire month. I was scared as to how my mother would respond to my father sending me money. Even though I was scared of my mother's reaction, a part of me felt carefree; my mother would not have to worry about paying for anything during the pandemic. The amount of money he sent was nothing to him, but to my mother and I, it was life changing.

My father was more than happy to help us. However, a part of me felt like he was mostly doing it to help sooth his own ego after leaving my mother and I. I was a little frustrated; it was unfair that my siblings grew up with money and never had to worry about making ends meet but my mother suffered to raise me and push me through school.

For so many people right now, the pandemic is an opportunity to get closer to their parents. Even with all the money my father was sending over, I would trade it all in a heartbeat to have had him in my life. When I was younger I used to cry when I would see the other kids, especially my cousins, with their dads. I never had the experience I once longed for. Now seventeen, I have forgiven him. I am thankful to have someone like my father to fall back on when things get tough. A lot of people do not have that kind of privilege.

But dad? We can't go outside anymore. But the door is still open.

Four

By Carlos Moreno

I have been constantly reminding myself that we are all quarantined in order to keep ourselves healthy. I have not thought of much else during this lockdown besides that. Obviously, I want to be able to go see my family and friends, but I also want to make sure everyone stays safe.

Before the quarantine began, my mom had already planned a gender reveal for my aunt's first child. The venue, guest list, and decorations were already set way in advance. All we needed was for the day to come. Once everyone was forced to begin social distancing, it was obvious that the party was off. My aunt and uncle were upset because it was supposed to be a special occasion for the beginning of their nuclear family. Someone who seemed even more bothered was my mom. She worked hard to plan the reveal detail by detail and had finally gotten everything together.

After some thinking, I realized that the show could, in fact, go on, but by a different set of rules. My idea was completely original. I suggested that we could have a social-distancing gender reveal. I drew out an entire diagram on how it could be set up on the back of a random paper. There was a big, vacant parking lot a few towns over that was perfect. Everyone who was invited would park around the sides, and my aunt and uncle would park in the center. At first, I thought it would just be a helpful suggestion. When I proposed my plan to my mom, however, she seemed intrigued, but told me that it was not reasonable because people would still be too close to each other. She did have a valid point. The way she pictured it, it was still a normal party. That was until I showed her my diagram of the parking lot and twenty poorly hand-drawn cars. It looked like a third-grade art project, but apparently it was good enough. To my surprise, my mom loved the idea. She called my aunt right away and pitched my idea to her. She loved it even more than my mom did. The new date was set for April 12th. Everyone would drive to the P.C Richard & Son parking lot, park around the edges, and remain in their cars.

When my family arrived, it was way bigger than I could have imagined. There were thirty-six cars lined up, decorated in all types of pink and blue decorations.

There were balloons, confetti, paint, and streamers. It was nice to see how many people came out to support my aunt and uncle. It was as if every branch of the family tree was being represented in that lot. When everyone was settled, my aunt and uncle brought out two huge smoke cannons. Everyone in the lot opened their windows and began the countdown. Suddenly, a police car rolled into the lot and stopped next to my car. Everyone froze with uncertainty. The officer then waved at my dad and took out his phone to record. We were not in any type of trouble, he just wanted to be there for the show. My aunt and uncle got back in position and the countdown began once more. Then, with a huge boom, the smoke fired out of the cannons. It's a boy! My uncle threw the cannon and started running and jumping around the lot. Everyone else was beeping their horns and screaming. I took a minute and looked around. I saw all my relatives wearing masks inside of their cars. Even though we had to be separated from each other, there was still a feeling of togetherness. I smiled and thought about the fact that not even a global pandemic could stop my family from having a good time together as one.

Five

By Ashley Galvez-Recinos

Five. Five members of my family caught Corona. Five members of my family were in danger. Five members of my family were the victims of people being selfish and not staying inside. Five members of my family were sent to the hospital. Five members of my family caught Corona.

That we know of.

Six

By Saned Ziyadeh

For as long as I can remember, I always wanted to get a job to help my family. Now, because of COVID, I have a job that could hurt my family.

Before the pandemic started, I really wanted to get a job to help both my family and I financially. I decided to apply to a job at a local pharmacy because it was one of the only places that were hiring. The next morning, I received a call and, soon after, I was granted an interview. The following day I began working. After working my first day I felt good. I was excited to keep working and make more money.

The next day I was happy to go into work. After clocking in and working up front on the register, I heard terrible news: my coworker told me that one of the other workers felt extremely sick. I was working with him the day before and I was scared. I thought that I was going to get the virus from him and spread it to my family. I felt selfish. I did not think of what getting sick could do to my family. I did not realize that if I get sick and get my family sick it would be very bad. I feel trapped in my job. I feel like I cannot escape. Every day that I have to go to work, anxiety eats me alive. When I first got the job, I was happy that I was able to help my family financially. I was going to get money. Now all I can think about is how much that cost.

Seven

By Jesus Pena

When things first started, nobody on the team took this new virus seriously. We were all frustrated that we wouldn't be able to play our first scrimmage or the games we had scheduled within the next two weeks, but we thought, "Oh well, it's just two weeks. It'll pass by quickly and in the meantime, at least we get a break from school."

"Social distancing," wasn't our main concern. Unbeknownst to our coaches, the baseball team decided to keep meeting up and practicing. We thought that since other teams were going to be home resting, we could be working and gaining an advantage over them by playing while we weren't supposed to. We believed the virus was real, we just didn't believe we would get it; I didn't believe Coach would get it.

Just five days after the closing of all Bergen County schools, Coach Jano and the athletic director were spamming my phone on a gloomy Monday morning. I had just woken up and had that morning voice teenagers have when they're sleep deprived. "Jesus, we have to talk to you and the team. Can you get everyone to join our video chat within the next 5 minutes?" I agreed to the impossible task of getting fifteen teenagers to wake up for a random call. Time passed and the news was finally broken to us: "Coach Ben passed away from the virus early this morning. He had been battling it for some days now and he didn't make it. This virus is real, you guys need to take it seriously. Stay home. Stay safe. Follow the guidelines in place so that hopefully one day soon, we can meet safely and really mourn his death together as a family."

I froze, and my initial instinct was to think they were joking, but I noticed the tears in their eyes, the raspiness of their voice, and the way their noses sniffled.

He's gone.

I immediately asked for more details and as I got answers, all I could picture was all of the memes, all of the player-held practices, and all of the unnecessary late-night food runs I made. The virus that nobody on the team feared had just taken the most valuable and invincible piece it had: Coach Ben. Coach Ben was inspirational, a motivation to all his players, as well as a mentor to everyone he met. He gave no excuses, and displayed 110% effort in everything he did, whether he was screaming to "go for two," or instructing his young students in the classroom. Most of all, he was loved; that's who this virus took from us.

The passing of Coach led not only the team, but to other students at our high school to take this virus seriously. No more unnecessary trips to get food. No more meeting up with friends to say, "Hey, what's up?" This became inevitable. This became real. More real than anything anyone on the team has had to deal with; anything I've had to deal with. I keep thinking that one day, perhaps, I'll round third base again and see him standing there: waving me home.

Eight

By Ashley Garcia

D o you know what isn't fair? Not being able to be with the person who has always been by your side when they are dying, and then to go to their funeral via Zoom. My grandfather has always been one of my biggest fans and supporters. He was always there to congratulate me on my accomplishments and tell me that it's okay whenever I failed. He fought a long, hard battle against cancer for many years. He went through countless treatments and surgeries so that he could live just a little longer. Then he died just like that.

I feel so much anger because of everyone who decides to go out and be around a lot of people during this time of crisis. Everyone in my family, including me, *chose* to stay home because we did not want to risk him catching anything. I did everything in my power to make sure I wouldn't get him sick because I heard all the stories about how people died all alone in the hospitals and I did not want that for my grandfather. One thing my grandfather always talked about was how he couldn't wait for my prom and graduation. He said he couldn't wait to see how beautiful I was going to look in my dress, and how proud he was going to be watching me get my diploma. But going to Applebee's was more important to some people than a man who loved.

Tuesday evening my grandfather passed away in a hospital. We weren't allowed to see him because they aren't letting anyone in the hospitals right now. I did not get to say goodbye to the man who has cherished me since the second I was born. My grandmother, who has been married to him for decades, did not get to kiss him goodbye. My father, who has worked hard to give him everything he could, couldn't hug him goodbye.

For his "funeral," my grandfather had a five-minute ceremony where only ten people were only allowed to stay for fifteen minutes because of social distancing. I was not part of the group that got to go see him one last time, and my grandmother was not even part of that group because she is quite old, and no one wanted her to risk going out. So, instead, the rest of the family and I watched through Zoom. My grandfather was an amazing person, and he deserved so much more than just that.

While some people don't see how serious this shit really is, I do. I'm going to keep staying home because I now know what it feels like to lose someone you truly love and adore, and to not be able to say goodbye. No one should go through the pain my family and I are going through right now because none of us were able to say goodbye. No one should go through the pain of dying alone in a hospital room, and not be able to be around everyone you love.

We were never meant to do this alone - this loving and living and grieving. We sure as hell weren't supposed to do the dying alone either.

Nine

By Emilio Figueroa

I thought I was invincible, but it wasn't me that I had to worry about. When the Coronavirus broke there was a sudden rise in cases. My grandfather was one of those cases.

My grandfather got Coronavirus during the third week of March. It all started when he said that his body was aching and that his back was hurting. My grandfather was old, but this had never happened to him before. So my grandfather decided to go to the hospital because of how bad it was getting. For a while, the doctors could not even test him.

After a week of being in the hospital, my grandfather was diagnosed with the Coronavirus. My mother was devastated, but I didn't know how to react. Fear started to take over. The terror of not knowing what will happen is what eats you from the inside out and becomes the only thing you can think about.

Days turned into about three and a half weeks. He was able to use his phone while he was in the hospital, so my mother would call him every single day to check up on him. This was the only way we could connect - to help us get through the pain he was enduring. I will never forget the pain in my grandfather's voice whenever we spoke on the phone.

I know he would want to see me succeed and have a bright future. I decided to work even harder in school and try to suppress my feelings about the situation. In the end, I believe I've become a strong, young man.

I just wish it didn't have to come at the cost of a strong, old one.

Ten

By Dorothy and Jamie Andersen

Jamie,

My English teacher asked the class to write a memoir about our last 5 weeks at home because of the Coronavirus pandemic. I started to write about what I missed out on. Missing out on my senior year sucks: no softball, no awards dinners, no prom, and no graduation, too. But then I started to think about you. Over the past 5 weeks you have been working non-stop at either the Cliffside Park EMS as an EMT or at St. Joseph's Hospital as a nursing assistant on the Covid -19 critical care unit. And that's in addition to all the homework you have been doing for your nursing classes.

I worry about you. I toss and turn in my bed. You are constantly risking your life to care for someone with the Coronavirus. What happens if you are exposed and something happens to you? I worry that if you get sick, will we get sick too? I watch these videos online where nurses are talking about what they are going through right now. They are struggling, they are crying and breaking down but when you come home, you don't say anything. You normally talk to me about your day, you tell me about the people you cared for and saved. Now nothing!

I am worried about you. I know we don't always agree on everything and sometimes we fight. But you are my big sister and you can always talk to me about whatever is bothering you. You have always taken care of me and guided me.

You are my hero. You always were but especially now. You are the reason I want to be a nurse, too. So please talk to me because I see the tears in your eyes, and it scares me.

I love you always even when I am being the biggest pain in your ass,
Dorothy

Dottie,

Sorry it took two days to write you back, but it's been so busy here at work and I really had to think about what I wanted to say. I guess what I need to say is that I love you with all my heart and have since the day you came home. You were always such a pain in the ass as a little kid but now that we are both older we are able to talk to each other and confide our secrets to each other - especially the ones we want to keep from mom! :)

It hasn't been easy these past five weeks; I have never been more scared to answer a call in the ambulance because I never know what is going to happen. The state has given us so many different rules to follow now. We have been told to gown up for every 911 call. We have been told to stand at the door and ask questions. The people I have seen have been so sick - I have never seen it this bad before and I feel horrible because I can't even do anything for them. It's horrible to watch family stand by the ambulance as they watch us put their loved one in the ambulance not knowing if they are ever going to see them alive again. It tears me up every time.

I think it's the worst when I have to go to work at the hospital. Before the pandemic, all my patients in my critical care unit were normally awake - they were sick, but not like now. Now, all my patients are Covid positive and they are all on ventilators. They are dying and it doesn't seem like our best is ever enough! Last night I watched a man not much older than me just stare at me every time we went into his room with tears in his eyes. I know he was scared and so was I! It took all my courage to not cry right there in front of him.

I don't want you to worry about me, I am fine. I have my co-workers at the EMS center and the hospital to speak to. We talk, we cry, and we hold each other when we have to. Don't be afraid of me getting sick, I am wearing all the proper equipment, all the time.

I am so proud of you; of the girl you've become! I know this sucks for you because you were supposed to be spending this time on the softball field with your friends and going to prom in your beautiful dress. I looked forward to driving you to prom in the Jaguar as your chauffeur. But don't worry: one way or another you will have your graduation and you will get to wear that dress!

Love you now and always,
Jamie

Eleven

By Emily Morel

Chew on this: Food is the thing I think most about. Who doesn't think about food? Before the quarantine, I would eat one meal and immediately start thinking about what I would be eating for the next meal. Most days, I would eat five meals and many snacks in between. I ate when I was hungry, of course, but I also ate when I was sad, when I was angry, when I was anxious, when I was bored, and when I felt lonely. At the end of the day, food means more to me than anything in the world; it provided me with company, fuel, and gave me something to do. Overeating left me feeling extremely full when I went to bed, causing me to take hours to fall asleep.

In the second week after school closures due to Coronavirus, I found myself unable to eat the same amount of food I was once eating. My mom did not want my siblings and me to eat the food as fast as we usually did. We went out for groceries every weekend before quarantine because of how fast food went in our household, so this new regulation limited how much food I ate throughout the day. One night, as I was trying to fall asleep, I saw a YouTube video on intermittent fasting. Intermittent fasting is having a certain amount of time in which one does not take in any calories. After the fasting period, one is able to eat food for a certain number of hours: the "eating window." I was shocked when I heard that some people fast for *days*. Although food was something I was constantly thinking about, giving intermittent fasting a try was something I had to consider due to the limited amount of food I could eat during quarantine. Grocery shopping every weekend quickly changed to every three weeks in order to reduce exposure to other people, and I stopped going to work where I would eat food to kill time.

After watching the video, I decided to apply the 16:8 method to my daily lifestyle, allowing for a 16-hour fast with an 8-hour eating window. The first day was difficult. I kept looking at my phone every five minutes hoping that the clock would move faster. Water is recommended to curb hunger throughout the fasting window, so I drank a lot more water than what I was used to. Once it was twelve o'clock, I ate immediately. String cheese, yogurt, sausage, chicken, I did not care what I ate as long as I was eating something. During the eating window it is recommended to eat all the necessary nutrients you need to keep your body healthy during the fasting period, something I was not doing.

As the days went on, it was getting a lot easier to get through the fasting periods without feeling irritable due to hunger. When I ate, I ate things that made my body feel good throughout the day. I started eating intuitively and ate until I genuinely felt full. My entire philosophy about food has changed completely during the past couple of weeks. Food was once a crutch I used to hold myself up when I was in a bad place, something that brought me good feelings but only temporarily. The eating pattern I have set myself up with over the past couple of weeks has taught me that food is so much more. Eating should be an activity one seeks out in order to fuel the body. Not only has my relationship with food changed, but I feel a lot less tired now than how I used to feel. The eating pattern even gave my body enough time to rest and digest the food I ate throughout the day, something that was difficult when I was convinced my stomach was a bottomless pit. Instead of going to bed feeling like I was going to burst, I went to bed comfortably satiated.

In a way, I am grateful for the time spent indoors during the quarantine. Before I stopped going to work, most of my income went towards purchasing food. *A lot* of food. I would drive to the McDonald's drive-through and in one sitting I enjoyed two salty meals which *had* to be followed up with a dozen cookies. Fast food restaurants are still open during the pandemic, but losing my own personal income eliminates the financial freedom I once had to buy an excess amount of unhealthy food. Staying at home all day has allowed me to focus on my digestive health and my relationship with food. What I know now is that food does not control the way I live my life and how I deal with my feelings.

Twelve

By Jasmin Levia

A lot of people are with their families right now, but I chose not to be. Months ago, I decided to stay with my friends for quarantine.

This all started when I bumped into my friends at the mall before anybody really knew the extent of the pandemic. I had not seen my friends in over a year and I slept over that same night. The next day came and I thought I should just stay here until the virus passed. We both made sure it was ok with our parents and, once we got approval, we picked up more clothes and any necessities. I thought that this was a perfect time to catch up and bond with my friends. Even though I would be away I only imagined being away for a couple of weeks and no one would mind me staying that long. Years ago, I had been on vacation with her for about two weeks, so I was used to being away for some time. I said bye to everyone and thought it won't be long until I saw them again. Days turned into weeks which turned into months. I realized I won't be home soon.

While I am here, I still have chores and responsibilities. I have my own bed which I need to make. I have my own bathroom necessities like shampoo and such and if they run out I buy more. They also make some meals for me, but I still need to buy groceries and make meals for myself when I get hungry. When my clothes start piling up, I have to do laundry and I have a schedule for when I can do it. I do not have everything given to me but am getting used to being treated like an adult.

The biggest chore, though, is being away. For over a month, the only communication I have with my family is over the phone. I cannot go back and visit whenever I please to minimize the spread of any germs. It is different when you cannot be with your family every minute and you miss some funny moments with them. I cannot see everything they are doing. We are under two different roofs and I can't hug them. Everyone gets caught up in their own lives, either with work or chores.

After a while, I started thinking about going back, but I don't have a license. My best option was to go back by Uber. I wanted to go on my own without my friends knowing. Being away for so long is fun at first but, after a while, I felt like a part of me was missing. I have been with my family for so long that being this distant breaks me little by little. Finally, I realized I cannot go back just for their safety, especially because I live (used to live?) with my grandparents. I realized that the cost of not seeing them is not as important as keeping them safe for the time being.

Never in my wildest dreams did I ever think I would have to choose to not see my parents and grandparents. Truth is, I never knew how hard it would be to give up a family. But, then, I never thought I would find one either.

Thirteen

By Yariza Orellana

As a student who is in the top ten of her senior class, you can imagine how excited I was when I received a full ride to Penn State University – a dream school I longed to go to. I felt overwhelmed because my hard work and sleepless nights throughout high school finally paid off. I was over the moon with excitement. But somehow during the middle of my senior year that excitement quickly turned into anxiety and sadness.

Somehow, somewhere, I got thrown into jail.

When COVID-19 hit my area, I had to start quarantining at home. I had to face the fact that I could no longer enjoy or celebrate my accomplishments with my friends and family without the fear of catching the virus.

I've been in quarantine for about a month now, and it has totally turned my world upside down. I usually spend my week running from school to track practice to piano class to church running errands for my parents. Ever since COVID-19 hit my area, I went from being outside all day to barely getting to go out to my backyard. It feels like I'm a prisoner who's only allowed to go into the courtyard for a short period of time.

Online school isn't the same because my friends aren't around me to make my classes more fun. I sit at my kitchen table every day from 8 A.M. until 12 P.M. all by myself. I do feel really sad at times. Not because I am physically alone - I have siblings at home - but because it's different than having people around me who are just as excited about senior year as I am. I feel so unmotivated to do anything and regret ever saying "I don't want to go to school today." I would do anything to be able to walk in Cliffside Park High School's hallway, sit in a classroom, and learn about literally anything.

It hurts me the most when I realize I've lost so many people around me because of COVID-19 to the point where I have lost count. I'm not even surprised anymore to hear that someone else I know has died. I am 17-years-old. I should *not* be acting as if another death is not surprising. But because of isolation, my numbness to the loss of family will probably continue. I've remained inside and cannot say goodbye to the people who mean the most to me. I truly feel like I've been imprisoned physically and emotionally, and it kills me to have to accept the fact that, if and when everything does go back to normal, I will not see a number of family again. I'm trapped inside – literally and figuratively– with nothing but pain and the memory of each of my family members.

Somehow, somewhere, I got thrown into jail.

Tomorrow, I will wake up, and choose once again to remain here.

Fourteen

By Luis Peralta

O nce, when I was young, I saw a tombstone with no name or date. It just read "Why?"

On Thursday, March 26th at approximately 10:00 pm, my mom received a devastating call from Ecuador: my uncle had lost his battle against Coronavirus. My mom nearly dropped the phone crying, screaming from the bottom of her lungs as she realized she had lost her older brother. I have never witnessed such a heartbreaking sight, and I hope to never see that again. Although I cannot compare my pain to the pain my mom was going through, I did not know how to keep myself strong. His absence left my mind blank and my heart aching, not knowing how it could get better.

What bothered me even more was that we had to endure our family pain in a whole different way. There was no seeing each other, no hugs, no crying or praying together. It made this loss feel so lonely and dreadful. These long, sad days my phone was no longer a distraction and my schoolwork was no longer a priority. With nowhere else to turn, the quarantine circumstances forced us to grieve online in daily Zoom meetings. That was the only way my family and I were able to find comfort and closure as we dealt with his death. Honestly, it still did not seem fair. Why did we have to overcome this pain on our own, without the physical presence and support of the rest of our family? That question will never be answered.

"Why?"

Fifteen

By Brandon Montalvo

In the beginning, it looked like this: Online school with unlimited snacks, sitting in your pajamas, all while playing PS4 all day. It was like the greatest Sunday ever, and we got to experience it every day. In the end, it goes like this: wake up for school. Attend classes from 8:00 am till noon. Eat breakfast, do homework, shower, play video games until 4:00 am. Repeat. When did life become a never ending and depressing Sunday?

Sixteen

By Kelly and Chelsea Chucaralao

Dear Chelsea,

I think we already know I don't want to deal with you *at all* during this quarantine. Just to be frank [If you don't know what that means- it's like saying straightforward] I know our personalities don't bode well for us in this house. Someone said, "This place ain't big enough for the two of us!" Maybe this letter will help clear things up: we each will have our own things like separate bunks and electronics. There shouldn't be a reason as to why you're on *my* bed and leaving a bunch of crumbs from *your* snacks. I don't want us fighting over a problem that you could've prevented. Secondly, that attitude of yours needs to switch up right now before I actually take it out of you.

I found out Dad is letting me work in Tío's room because he's still in Washington. So I'm taking that offer without a doubt just to be away from a toxic quarantine. No offense, but I would rather be alone than be stuck with you for an entire day. If dad's giving me this option, bet my life that I'll take it. I'm sorry that you'll get stuck with mom and her attitude. Maybe you two will bond over that because I know I'm going to escape from you guys.

From your sister,
Kelly
P.S. If I catch you eating on my bed, don't be surprised when I sucker-punch your face.

Dear Kelly,

I can't be stuck with you. When I go to the kitchen for a snack, we have to share. When I want to do something, you respond, "Not really, no." When we're bored, you put Netflix on the TV but constantly watch *Criminal Minds*. Life is hard when you're here. It bothers me when you don't do anything. Sometimes you get mad, but five minutes later, it's like nothing happened. I mean, at least we jam to the same songs, right? I love you, but you gotta chill.

Love,
Chelsea

Dear Chelsea,

So we're about fourteen days into quarantine. We've gone out to buy our groceries every Sunday and do laundry once a week. I want to thank you for going with mom and I because I know I wouldn't handle being alone with her. Her attitude isn't something I want to deal with; she drives me crazy. Luckily, with you coming it makes running errands more comfortable and unpredictable. The only thing that makes me want to hit you across the head with a bat is when you touch a bunch of items. Stop doing that.

My favorite run was the day we bought two tubs of chocolate & vanilla ice cream. Mom didn't seem to notice we bought two of the same flavors! Also, and this needs to be said, the amount of waffles we've had every week is extreme. Yes, they are delicious and thank you for putting in the time to make me some, but I think I'll eat cereal here and there.

In a surprising turn of events, Mom and Dad decided to make a celebration for my birthday. I originally had a whole plan to go out with my friends and come home to spend a bit of time with you and our parents. Under the circumstances, I'm quite happy I had all of you guys to be here for my birthday. I wanted to turn eighteen and be outside. At least I got to spend the majority of that day with you.

Love your sister,
Kelly

Dear Kelly,

Haven't seen you in forever! This month we've been close - almost inseparable from each other. I missed this. Every day we play Uno together with dad. And it's like we don't care if we share the same snacks. Now, when I tell you my dreams, you actually listen to me, which is cool and I appreciate it. Thank you! I feel lucky as cheese to have a sister like you! I remember when we used to fight over who washed the dishes, but now we don't even care. You know when I cook, you wash them. I love spending time with you!

Yours truly,
Chelsea

Dear Chelsea,

I'm going to cut to the chase here: I'm glad we've spent quarantine together. Although it feels as if we're trapped in this house, I'm happy that I have someone to be stuck with. I can't imagine being left to face mom on my own. I found it hilarious when we were driving with mom in the car. You and I were craving ice cream, and we asked her to buy some in a store. Even though I was driving, I could feel her eyes glaring at us. She started questioning us about buying two tubs a while back. By the time we got out of the car to go into the store, we laughed uncontrollably.

A couple nights ago, we couldn't go to sleep because of our horrible sleep schedules. Instead of trying to relax, we started making jokes. We didn't have to physically see each other to imagine our reactions. You fell asleep about an hour later [weak] and I finally closed my eyes around 3:00 am. I managed to wake up in the morning for class. You were already sitting in the chair. There hasn't been a day where we don't laugh or make comments about the class we're in.

I am grateful about having a sister like you in my life. Although you always got on my nerves before this quarantine, I think this gave us a chance to really connect with one another. I'm not sure how long we'll be stuck at home, but I'm happy to be with someone who makes me laugh and keeps me company.

From the *Uno* Master,
Kelly

Dear Kelly,
    Yeah, I love you too.

From,
Chelsea

Seventeen

By Jaylene Suarez

Breathe in and breathe out, I told myself. For the majority of the last two weeks, I have been extremely sick. It was different from any other time I have been sick, and I realized this right from the start. I stayed in bed for the first couple of days and didn't feel any sort of recovery, so I tried to carry on with my normal routine. However, each day I would feel more pain caused by my cough.

I got out of bed, went to get a bottle of water, and walked to the living room where my mom had the tv on at a low volume. The news was giving an update on COVID-19. The updates included new cases, more deaths, and the repetitive announcement of warning symptoms. Hearing the news, I allowed my mind to begin to wander down an infinite spiral of negative thoughts. The thoughts I had been having were putting me into a panicked state.

I woke up trying not to breathe in too hard because it would set off the coughing. I moved to sit up and was shot through by an agonizing pain in my ribs. I checked my phone while still laying down, switching between the different social media platforms. On Twitter, I saw graphs representing the rapidly increasing cases which set me into overdrive. I tried to sit up again but couldn't and ended up coughing, sending the pain in my ribs to an unbearable level. With no fight, I began to think I would never get over this illness. I was terrified. My mind raced with countless thoughts: *If I didn't have it were my chances of getting it higher? If I got COVID-19 or had it, how badly would I be affected? If I got it bad, would I end up only being able to see my mom through a screen? Would I get to go to college and start a family, or would I meet my end in a hospital room alone?*

I woke up due to the sudden coughing and felt like no air could get to my lungs. I ran out of my bedroom, ending up in the kitchen, trying so intensely just to breathe. I ended up vomiting, and I leaned against the counter for a while and cried. Whatever I had was going to take me out. My mom, who had gone grocery shopping, could have brought something that was contaminated. The last days of my life could be near because of a box of Life cereal.

I needed to remain calm and present. Breathe in and out. I was letting fear control me. The numbers for COVID-19 cases were still rising, but they would come down. Like the pain I had been feeling in my ribs would ease, so would everything else.

Breathe in and breathe out, I told myself. Breathe in and breathe out.

Eighteen

By Emely Orbea

I look at myself in the mirror. *I'm essential,* I think. It's time for work.

A month ago, it was all calm and normal. No cases of COVID-19 were found where we lived. All was calm at ACME. I was a regular high school student working about 20 hours a week. I had regular four to five-hour shifts. I easily made about $150-$200 a week. It was so simple.

By the second week of March, my job turned into complete chaos. The line wrapped around the store as people filled their carts with things to keep them home for two weeks. I came into work not ready for what was going to happen. I remember those three days: March 12th, 13th and 14th. I worked 30 hours alone in those three days. I wore gloves to protect myself, thinking that one of the thousands of customers that came in that day could have had the virus. I was worn down and exhausted as our store was wiped clean of every item people needed to survive. I went home that Saturday afraid - terrified that I could have gotten the virus. I was exhausted but still had to wrap my head around the fact that I did not have a single day off the following week. One week later, I went to get tested, and three days after that I came back negative. I was surprised.

I had a choice to make: Do I want to go to work, or do I want to keep myself safe? Eventually, I wanted to help people. I made the right decision. I became an essential worker. I would have never thought a grocery store clerk would be considered essential. To be honest, yes we supply people with food, but that's normal. In a time like this, however, supplying people with food is golden. I get a "thank you" almost twenty times a day. I usually never got tips at ACME, or even compliments, but now, my day is filled with those. I chose to go to work to supply people with what they need to stay home. Currently, I work 40 hours a week. I work from 3:00 pm until closing every day, ensuring that the people, and the store itself, are pleased.

I fear every day that I'm going to come home with the virus and infect my parents. I am very stressed, and I am behind on a lot of work for my classes. The anxiety that hits me every day before work is something

I can't explain. I shouldn't be afraid to go to work. I take a deep breath before leaving my house. I can't worry about that now. I look at myself in the mirror and think *I'm essential.* It's time for work.

Nineteen

By Fatima Jamil

March 3, 2020: Noon

Instead of buying essentials for our home, my family and I all decided to go to the mall. My mother and I were shopping together getting ready for a vacation. We were having the time of our lives, talking, laughing, and trying on items of clothing. We did not know that our life would become crashing down in a couple minutes.

March 3, 2020: 4:09 pm

My aunt decided to call us. My mother and I were on separate sides of the store, so I did not know she got a call. I was grabbing items and putting it in my cart when I heard yelling. I began to look around to see who this person was screaming, not knowing it was my mother. She came running towards me, "He died, he died, someone shot him, he died!" She finally let out the name and tears began to fall out of my eyes. My cousin, who was like an older brother to me, was gone. I did not believe my mom at first - I was in denial. We rushed back to the car with my father and brothers to drive home. The car ride was filled with screams and crying. My arms went numb, my chest was hurting, I was unable to breath, tears all over my face. I thought I was going to have a heart attack.

March 4, 2020

The next morning both my parents and uncles left for Oregon to attend his funeral. My brothers and I stayed home alone, still in denial that this was happening. We were all heartbroken that we lost someone that was like a brother to us, but now we had something else to worry about: Our parents had a chance of getting the virus. All of us were terrified that one of them would get it.

March 5, 2020

My father flew back from Oregon and came home safely. My mother decided to stay with her sister for a couple weeks to help her with everything that was going on.

March 13, 2020

My mother was supposed to come back home on March 16, but with the virus spreading, we changed the flight for her to come back earlier. I missed my mother so much; not having my best friend at this tough time was very hard to get through. When she arrived, she was a bit off. I noticed that there was something wrong but decided not to question her about it.

March 15, 2020

My mother starts coughing very frequently. Her body begins to ache. A fever rose and she could no longer taste nor smell. I did not want to believe that she had caught the virus. My family and I began to worry, her symptoms were becoming worse and we wanted to take her to the hospital. She did not let us. She thought it would get worse if she went. We decided to quarantine her in one of the bedrooms.

March 20, 2020

My brother begins to cough and lose his senses of taste and smell. He was also having body aches, but there was not a high fever. We all thought it was an early stage of the virus.

March 22, 2020

My brother's symptoms begin to get worse. He decides to quarantine himself in his bedroom.

March 30, 2020

My mother begins to feel better. She is able to taste and smell again. Her fever and body aches are gone. We are so happy and hoping the same for my brother.

April 1, 2020

My brother begins to feel better. His symptoms were not as bad as my mother's.

April 5, 2020

We begin to hear that several people in our neighborhood are getting infected. They were all very close friends to us. One of them passes away.

April 10, 2020

A woman that treated my mother like another daughter gets infected by the virus. She has been unconscious in the hospital for weeks. The days run into each other. All the days are the same. There are no more days.

Twenty

By Olivia Peterson

It was a few days into quarantine. It was about 5:00 am when I heard my mom wake up. She had a fever.

The next morning, she was still sick, but only with a fever. I started to become a little scared because I was thinking it was Coronavirus, but I was not sure. For the next few days my mom stayed quarantined in her room just in case. I came in little contact with my mom during that week, only making her soup and leaving it outside her door. She wore gloves and a mask when she did leave her room to keep my brother and I safe while she waited for the results.

It took a whole week for the results to come back. By the time she got her results, she was feeling much better. However, she tested positive for Coronavirus. I was glad she was feeling better and hoped the virus was completely gone from our home.

About three days after my mom received her results, I woke up one morning feeling a little sick. Mostly I just felt weak. I noticed my sense of taste and smell were completely gone. This first day I felt too weak to really move around, so I just stayed in my room. It almost felt as if I was hallucinating and was moving in slow motion. I tried to take a shower hoping it would make me feel a little better, but I started to feel extremely nauseous and thought I was going to pass out.

Other than that first day when I felt weak and first noticed I couldn't taste or smell, I mostly felt fine. I still did my schoolwork and did not feel weak at all. I continued with my days like normal, except I didn't really enjoy eating because food tasted like nothing. I also slept more than usual.

After five days of not being able to taste or smell, my parents knew it wasn't just allergies and thought it was a good idea that I get tested. I told them there was really no point to getting tested because the results took a while for my mom to get back so it would probably take a while to get mine back as well. Also, if I was tested positive, I would just have to stay in my room, which is what I was doing anyway. They agreed and decided to just let time play out.

Almost two weeks after I lost my taste and smell, both finally started to come back. I was relieved it didn't get any worse than that. Some cases are deadly, and others are very minor. But now here's the question: Did I have COVID or didn't I? What if I'm safe?

What if I'm not?

Twenty-One

By Arslan Hashmi

On March 1, I was in New York City on a rooftop celebrating my cousin Sulaiman's 18th birthday. Partying with some of my best friends, I felt complete and fulfilled. I felt like I didn't need anything else. I was laughing; I was happy. I was having one of the best times of my life. Sulaiman's party ended. Then the party *really ended.*

Quarantine, due to Covid-19, kept me in a one-bedroom apartment with an 86-year-old woman, my grandma. She was the only person I could interact and communicate with in-person. We do - well, we do *not* share a lot in common. I cannot talk to her about Nav's upcoming album or about Thomas Shelby in *The Peaky Blinders*. After two weeks in quarantine, the consequences of it really got to me. The lack of face-to-face interactions led me into feeling very alone and depressed.

How I felt in isolation was the complete opposite of how I felt during the rooftop birthday party. While in quarantine, I felt betrayed by the world around me. I was hurting mentally and physically. The world took the one thing that motivated me to get up in the morning: human interaction. As humans, we live by interacting with the people and the world around us. If we lose that, like I did, we cannot function properly. In addition to feeling betrayed, I felt like I was lost in the world; I felt like I was drowning in darkness. Before, I would go talk to mom or my best friend face-to-face to figure out and solve my problems. In quarantine, however, I had to talk to them on the phone or text them to address my problems, which never worked. As a result, my problems kept piling up until I could not carry them any longer.

Soon, I started to get bored of doing the things I loved. In quarantine, I had plenty of time to do whatever my heart desired. In the beginning, this was amazing because it meant I could wake up at 2 p.m. and play *Warzone* or *Fortnite* for five to six hours straight without any consequences. However, like all parties, the freedom wore out quickly. Since I was playing video games for hours every day, they got boring very quickly. This happened with almost everything I loved. This was the lowest I ever felt. Wherever I turned, loneliness, depression, and fear were staring right at me; I could not escape them. I knew they had grown greater than me and I had to do something to stay sane.

Whenever faced with an obstacle, I try to plan out a solution. I knew if I did not plan a solution, I would go down a hole that I could not climb out of. I knew that the lack of in-person human interaction was the root of all my problems. Since I was not able to see and talk to people face-to-face, I needed to find something else that replaced human interaction. I had to experience the world and its people in a new way.

Soon, I got a piece of paper and started listing the different possibilities, such as drawing, photographing, reading, and sewing. Over the course of the first week, I tried every single one. First, I gave drawing a chance because it was easy, and I kind of liked it. I would draw random thoughts in my head onto a piece of paper. It was gratifying and relaxing at first. However, I did not have the patience to do it for a long period of time. So, I crossed out drawing. Then, I tried sewing with my grandma. That also failed because it was just boring. It required so much time and effort. Then, there were two: photographing and reading. I thought I was going to fail at reading, so I tried photography first. Taking pictures was fun;

however, I did not have many things to take pictures of because I was trapped in my one-bedroom apartment.

Finally, I had to try, gulp, reading. And, reader, I was none too thrilled. My whole life, I have hated books and everything regarding books. I never really see the point of reading. When I was young, my eyes used to water up and tears would come out whenever I tried reading anything. I thought books might help, even though I hated them throughout my whole life. I was desperate.

Soon, I would be reading for two to three hours every day. As I was reading through different books, all my problems disappeared. It kind of freaked me out a little, to be honest. I'm not sure if you are aware of this, but you can actually see the world through someone else's eyes in a book. Like, someone should put that on a poster.

After seeing my life turn around, I started to read more and more. Whenever I was bored, I would start reading. Whenever I needed to clear my mind, I would start reading. Whenever I needed to relax, I would start reading. Reading helped me learn about different people, places, and cultures without leaving my bed. Reading spiced up my whole life.

Now I know the truth: Sulaiman had a great party, but the man was no Gatsby. In books, it turns out, the party never stops.

Twenty-Two

By Jakelyn Reyes

When people say they are bored, what does that mean? Does it mean they can't find anything to do? Does it mean there is nothing to do? Does it mean deep inside ourselves we know we can give and do more, but we just choose not to? Is life boring? Are people boring? Am I boring? Can you be bored with too much time? Can you be bored in small pockets of time? We live in an entertainment saturated society, yet it seems we have never been as bored as we are now. Is that true? Is it because we all have too much free time now? Is it because we've never known what to do with the time we have?

Do people need distractions to not be bored? What about bad distractions? Can you be bored while you're also worried about a loved one's health? Maybe this pandemic could be an opportunity for these people not to be bored? Maybe boredom is a choice? Maybe everyone that is experiencing "boredom" in these times is doing so because they have chosen to be bored?

What about families? What about movies? What about Sunday dinners with those extra special desserts? What about bettering yourself? What about not letting boredom get the best of you during the quarantine? Can you choose to better yourself? Maybe you can come out of this wiser with a whole new outlook?

What about cooking, sitting, and having dinner together every night. Ooh, what about baking? Can you be bored baking desserts? Have bored people never heard of cookies, brownies, carrot cake, or banana bread?   What about *cheesecake*?

You ever hear of the little things? Do bored people know you can open up and be more expressive to your family and friends? Do they have a brother they can ask to get a water bottle? Can they make their dads breakfast? Do they know how to appreciate nothing? Surely, they know that we mustn't let boredom overpower us, right? Can boredom get the best of us? What is boredom, anyway?

Sorry, don't ask me. I'm just bored.

Twenty-Three

By Sumya Dotse

This virus was supposed to keep us apart. For me and my dad, though, it brought us closer together.

Before they started closing non-essential businesses, my dad was still working seven days a week. Since he works in a clothing store in New York, the state with the most cases, I was scared for him. Though many people were bored during this time, staying in a house with four other siblings there was always something happening. In those two weeks, I was still fine with staying in my house. My dad would come home, and we would all tell him, "You should stay, this is getting serious," but my dad is the type of person to work through anything even when he's sick. He even worked through the Superstorm Sandy, and some of the worst snow blizzards, so a virus wasn't going to stop him. After a while, though, it wasn't up to him any longer. Eventually, the government closed all non-essential businesses, and my father had to finally stop working and stay home. It was for the best.

I never got the chance to really have discussions or have deep one-to-one conversations with my dad because he was always working, and when he came home he would always be tired. This was understandable because of the days and hours he worked. Being home without leaving was a whole new thing for him. He couldn't even go to the gym, which he loved almost more than working. He made up his mind that if he couldn't go to the gym, he would bring the gym to himself. When he told me about what he was going to do I saw this as an opportunity to bond with him. I also like working out and going to the gym, so I asked my dad if I could help him out. Our first mission was to find an elliptical machine. We searched the web for the best type of elliptical for a decent price. It was a challenge, but we finally found one.

The place we were picking up the elliptical was far away and, because of the pandemic, we had to be cautious. We bought face masks and gloves, and we were on our way. Driving in the car listening to music gave us a chance to talk, and I learned that we are both big debaters. We love discussing topics and sharing our opinions, even though we didn't always agree.

Sharing these discussions was meaningful. When we arrived at the place, the two of us had to carry the elliptical to the van. It was very heavy but the two of us managed to carry it. Accomplishing that for us was just the start, and we felt like we made a real beginning. As days passed, my dad and I grew closer. Soon, we started looking for weights to buy. Even though the virus forced everyone to stay apart, being with my dad was the closest we had ever been. Every car ride bringing new gym equipment, the stronger our bond grew. The world may be miserable outside. But every few weeks, my dad and I are able to bring a little more happiness in.

Twenty-Four

By Jamie Garcia

I haven't loved myself for a while now. I used to, I think. Before quarantine, in the before times. Or maybe I just liked myself but never really loved myself. I don't know. I miss interacting with my friends and teachers. I miss being *loved.* How could I be loved and not love myself? I know and believe that I am loved by God in a way that exceeds all limits, and that if it were up to Him, he would treat me differently than I treat myself now that I'm alone. I started to notice this during quarantine. I can feel God's big love, but I wonder why he loves me so much. Because what I see is ugliness. I see a girl who has lost so much. This isn't something you know right off the bat, no! It's like when you get sick, and the first thing that happens are the small symptoms. That's what it's been like on quarantine. And my diagnosis turned out to be that

I have no love for myself. I don't hate myself, or wish myself ill, but I feel disgusted doing so little.

I wonder what I used to do when I was a child. I wonder if she could help me. I wonder if she would feel hurt if she read this. I wonder if I would crush her entire world if I told her this. I just don't see myself the way others see me, despite the fact that I believe that others see me in the most beautiful way. Maybe this is normal. My parents always said, "do it for yourself!" But I would always do it for them. I always did it for others. But it makes sense now, why I always sought to improve myself, and why I let myself go now that there is no school. I have to learn to love myself, and to be honest with myself. I don't really know what that looks like. I don't even know what that means.

Twenty-Five

By Talia Tobey

D id you ever love someone so much that you never want to see them again?

My family has been extremely cautious ever since COVID-19 broke out. The main reason why everyone in my house is sacrificing is for my grandmother. My grandmother is 74-years-old and has some medical conditions. Although she is in pretty good shape for her age, we are really worried for her. God forbid if she were to get the virus, none of us would be able to forgive ourselves. It takes one mistake; one "I'll be careful when I go out and won't touch anything." It should be easy to sacrifice your social life when it comes to putting those you love at risk. It seems like people won't ever understand that until they lose someone that they love.

Three of my family members had COVID-19 and are thankfully okay. My aunt, who I see often, had the virus. She was very scared; she couldn't be around my uncle and my cousins, her husband and her kids, and had to self-quarantine in her room for about three weeks. She had not gone out, or had physical contact with, anyone other than the people she lives with. My aunt assumed she caught the virus by touching her mail and not washing her hands after. Since then, she has successfully beat the virus and is back to spending time with her family during quarantine. My grandfather and his husband also got COVID-19. My grandpa's husband works at a medical facility, and he unfortunately brought it home to my grandpa. It is only the two of them living together, so they had to self-quarantine themselves when they both tested positive. A week and a half later, they both got tested again, and my grandpa tested negative, but his husband tested positive. They had to stay in separate rooms, and if they interacted with each other, they had to keep a distance and wear masks.

Although people in my family had the virus and we were extremely concerned, the main thing we wanted and needed was to stay away. It was hard to not be able to go and help them in person. Who would have ever thought that the biggest way you can help someone was by staying as far away from them as possible, that the biggest love I had to give wasn't a hug but a goodbye?

Twenty-Six

By Nelda Martinez

Well-meaning teachers have been telling me for years that every choice I make now will shape my future: my opportunities, my college, and even my career. I listened. What they didn't tell me, or what I didn't hear, was that there would be a clock. I always thought that I had all the time in the world. Then the universe gave me more time than I could handle, and I realized I had none.

College is one of the biggest and most important choices I'm ever going to make, a choice that could jumpstart my career and set my adult life in motion. There is a lot of planning that goes into choosing the perfect college, with dozens of different factors that I need to look into to help me decide. Would I want to commute or dorm? Which school would be better for me financially? Which school offers a better program for my major? Which school do I feel like I belong in? Would I consider playing a sport or getting a job?

These were things I could have thought about last year or in the fall, but I kept saying to myself, "I will just think about that tomorrow." I kept repeating that over and over, thinking I had so much time to plan. Before I knew it, however, I was on lockdown with no way of visiting campuses. Suddenly, I was unable to speak face-to-face with college admission officers or counselors. I am not able to see if I feel safe in a college environment, or if I am able to fit in with my peers.

It's not the same, sitting in front of a computer doing research and talking to people virtually, rather than being out there physically and seeing everything for myself. Someday soon, I will have to pick where to spend the next four years, and I will have to do it mostly blind. My entire life I was told to plan for tomorrow. I did. What nobody ever told me was what to do when tomorrow never comes.

Twenty-Seven

By Kataib Mohammed and Hazyza Deljanin

The 93rd Surah from the *Quran* begins like this: "By the morning brightness, by the night when it is calm! Your Lord has neither forsaken you, nor is He displeased with you."

This month, Muslims all around the world celebrate Ramadan, the ninth month of the Islamic calendar and a time to build a stronger connection to God. During Ramadan we normally attend daily mosque events and services, see friends and family, and give of ourselves to help those in need. It is a time of fasting, prayer, and community. In quarantine now because of the effects from COVID, Muslims in America and elsewhere must get by with just the first two.

FaceTiming is a good way to keep in touch with everyone, but it just doesn't feel right. With Ramadan almost being over and Eid right around the corner, it's going to feel weird without family. Eid is when families also come together to celebrate their month of fasting. Everyone cooks food, all the kids play, the teenagers gossip, and the parents hang out. It's a wholesome holiday where everyone is always happy. I'm upset that my family and I couldn't experience Ramadan together and now that it's coming to an end, I'm even more upset that we won't spend Eid as a family.

Before quarantine, my whole family would sometimes get together during Ramadan to have really big feasts where we would all break our fasts. Without community to look forward to, fasting itself has been more difficult than ever, as there is nothing to distract myself with. I am forced, for perhaps the first time, to truly look inward. In these quiet spaces, I hear the 93rd Surah: "Soon your Lord will give you [that with which] you will be pleased...and as for your Lord's blessing, proclaim it!"

Twenty-Eight

By Edson Almeida

O*ne step*, I remind myself. *Just one step.*

In December 2019 I got ACL reconstruction surgery. I went to therapy about three times a week and my recovery was going well, and fast. In March, I had an appointment with my doctor in New York City. In the hospital, everyone was taking extra caution. Even the receptionist who called my name to go to the room seemed to be scared to speak with me. But all the fear went away when my doctor told me that I would be able to start running under the supervision of a physical therapist. I remember that I was so excited. Six months after my injury, I would finally be able to run again. All this time I dreamed about the day I would get back on a soccer pitch and running was the first big step towards it.

Then Corona came. Most establishments closed, including my therapy. When I finally had the chance to make major progress towards playing soccer again, the virus made that progress impossible. Soon, I got very sick. My family and I all had symptoms of Coronavirus, including headaches, nausea, coughing, and body aches. I scheduled an online appointment with my doctor and she told me that we most likely did get the virus, but she could not test because none of the symptoms were fatal. The news was shocking. For about two weeks, I had to deal with a sickness that never went away. My joy of being able to run became a fear that I would not even be able to walk.

It was at that time that my knee began to hurt a lot. Going from intense workouts in therapy to no exercises at all became too much for my knee to handle. Between missing out on physical therapy and getting sick, my recovery had slowed to a literal grinding halt.

I decided to download an app and begin to take the steps I needed to myself. The first few days felt terrible. It was nearly impossible to do the exercises but, moreover, to stop whatever I was doing and spend one hour killing myself. Soon, however, working out raised my spirit in such a way that I looked forward to it every day. I felt good about my shape and my mind was a lot less distracted by all things going on around me. I was still not feeling 100%, but my knee started feeling a lot better.

Finally, I decided to call my therapist to see what I should do, and he cleared me to run. I was so excited that I went outside on the same day. I started with one step. Now, each day, I take several hundred.

Twenty-Nine

By Stephanie Valdez

My mom and I were in the kitchen making a traditional Dominican dish when we received a call from my aunt: she had the Coronavirus. We had to help and sprang into action immediately. We brought her family groceries. We helped pay their bills. We did this from the outside, from behind locked doors and boarded windows. How weak would love have to be, anyway, to not travel six feet?

Thirty

By Christian Orizabal

L ike great knights of old suiting up for battle, I was preparing for adventure. My armor, the clothes I chose for combat, felt like strangers to my skin after three weeks staying home in my pajamas. The weight of my shoes threw me off. I hadn't worn them since quarantine began so my feet felt imprisoned. My toes could no longer feel the carpeted floor of my room.

I was ready. For the first time in nearly a month, I was going *outside*.

I stood by the door ready to leave and I felt as if we were going out into the apocalypse. My mom gave me a whole bottle of hand sanitizer to carry and my dad grabbed a mask and a bag with a paper towel drenched in rubbing alcohol. My mom then told me and my four-year-old sister the following: Do not touch the walls in the hallway, use the hand sanitizer when we get in the car, don't touch your face, be careful when opening doors by using your sleeve or a piece of cloth to open a door. I opened the door of our apartment and walked down the hallway to get to the driveway with my sister and father behind me. I immediately felt off. I felt disgusted not being in the safe and clean environment that was our apartment. Too scared to touch anything, I opened the door to get to the driveway with my sweater sleeve and proceeded to walk to the car. The sunlight immediately blinded me and the breeze caught me by surprise.

During the car ride I was scared for my life. There were less people out on the streets than usual, but I would have imagined there would have been less cars as well. On the way down to Edgewater I passed by one of my friend's houses and began to think of all the fun times I had with him: When we could talk to each other in person in school. When we were able to hangout on the weekends.

We finally made it and I could see two people inside ordering from the window of the restaurant and a woman sat outside of the restaurant eating her fries. They were dragons whose breath was fire. My dad put on his mask and made his way inside while I stayed in the car with my sister.

My dad finally made his way back to the car and applied the hand sanitizer. The smell of fast food filled the air. My mouth began to water. Like brave knights before me in tales of great Grail quests, we had ventured forth from our home, familiar with but undaunted by danger. We had reached, at last, our final treasure.

A burger never tasted so good.

Thirty-One

By Victoria Ramos

My dad turns to me from his hospital bed. "Don't cry if I'm gone," he whispers, his voice hoarse. Tears well up in my eyes anyway. I wish hard to never have to hear those words again.

My father has had four heart attacks and was not supposed to survive his last. They run into each other now. The night of his near-fatal attack was so intense and traumatizing that feelings are all that remain, vague sense memories of trauma rather than concrete recollections. There he is on the bed. There I am on the floor. There were countless days where I stayed in the hospital by his side and watched him carefully. The days run into each other now, too.

Bringing Corona into my home would be life-threatening to my dad. I choose to stay inside so that I do not have to see my dad in a hospital bed, but I know I am not in control. I can't imagine losing my father. I have been a daddy's girl since the beginning, my first ever words calling for him. Losing him would be like losing a piece of who I am. My father is the reason why I want to chase my dreams of becoming a doctor.

My dad turns to me from his bed, aware of the pandemic raging outside. "Don't cry if I'm gone," he whispers, his voice hoarse. Tears well up in my eyes anyway. I wish what I wished before, only harder.

Thirty-Two

By Dilsy Gonzalez

My boyfriend doesn't like to take pictures. He says I'm too obsessed with trying to have a record of the moments we share rather than living in them. There's this one I have of the two of us - we're laying down in the park, looking up at the sky. I look at it now and remember what it was like to feel someone by my side. I remember feeling peaceful. I don't remember the exact day we took it. But I remember we were happy.

The pandemic has caused many conflicts in my life, but the most difficult one has been not being able to see my boyfriend. It is very difficult to be separated from someone who has spent a lot of time with you. It is a horrible feeling to not see that person every day. I miss being able to hug him, or see him, or be with him. Somehow, I went from being in a close relationship to a long distance one overnight. By being forced into quarantine, the world took someone very special away that made me feel complete.

Even though I talk to him every day, I still miss him. It's not the same talking to someone through a phone compared with talking to him in person. When I talk to him in person, I can see his facial expressions, feel his presence, and feel his warmth. Now that is gone.

Sometimes, my boyfriend and I talk to each other through the computer. Framed by a small box, he looks like a picture. My boyfriend doesn't like to take pictures. He says I'm too obsessed with trying to have a record of the moments we share rather than living in them.

Thirty-Three

By Emily Guadalupe Ventura

I remember feeling really sick a while back and I missed about two to three days of school. It was just a bad stomachache, but I felt fragile and weak. In four years, I had never missed a day of soccer before and, although I felt sick, something deep down made me feel guilty for not attending.

I returned to school after missing three days to mass confusion. The energy and atmosphere of the school was different. My teachers looked nervous and shared that they did not know if they would see us ever again. Deep down I knew they wouldn't, and that it was the last day I would be stepping through those doors.

As time in quarantine became longer and lonelier, I started to think a lot about my life but, no matter what path I would start on, my brain would always circle back to the one night I missed practice. I think of that day often because I never thought that would be my last. It would be the last time I would ever play with those girls and the last time we shared a field together. It was the last time I would be a part of something special I had helped build with those particular people.

I remember the moments we would stay after practice just to play together, the times we would complain when the coach wrapped up practice early. I remember one time the sky opened up and it poured down on us, but we kept going, laughing at the rain. I can feel how wet my cleats were and how heavy my clothes felt. I can hear the cries from my teammates, louder and more powerful than the thunder.

We often take things for granted. We walk around, going about our day, knowing that there will always be a tomorrow. But every practice is the last practice for someone, every day is the last day somewhere. What if today, this very moment, was our last day on this earth? Then what? Would we take all the missed opportunities, or would we leave them for the next person to take? Would we hate everything as much as we do now?

If I had known that the Coronavirus would start taking away everything I worked so hard for little by little I would have appreciated them a little more. I would not have missed that last practice. I would not have dogged the last sprint. Only if I knew that would be my last day.

But I didn't. And now, as much as I miss them, I know I have to say goodbye. But I also know that nothing is forever, that one day, perhaps, we will be back on the field, the girls whose joy was louder than thunder. I wouldn't miss it.

Thirty-Four

By Albert Gonzalez

By the fourth week of the quarantine it was official: I was a hostage. I wanted to go outside, but my parents wouldn't let me. Finally, I had enough. Having not seen the sun in a month, I was determined to argue with my parents until they relented. There was no way I could lose this argument. I had planned for every counter and knew how to respond.

For weeks, I kept re-reading my little speech multiple times, hoping that it was going to convince my parents to let me out. It took me some courage to go up to both of them and to start speaking, but in the end, I went to their room and I told them what was on my mind.

"Mom and Dad, I wanted to tell you guys this for a long time, but it could never come out of my mouth. I have wanted to go outside, but most importantly, I wanted to see my girlfriend one more time. I haven't seen her or the sun in two months and I think today is the day that it changes."

There was complete silence for about a minute. I felt very awkward.

My mother quickly replied with, "Pero mijo, it is too dangerous to go outside. What you see now is completely different than what you saw in the past few years. No one wants to leave their houses and every shop has the utmost security when it comes to masks and gloves. If you don't have either, they will force you to leave whether you like it or not. It's like a ghost town out there."

"All I want to do is see everyone one last time," I responded. "I will wear my gloves and my mask. I promise, but please, just let me go out. I beg of you."

Tears started to flow from my eyes and my parents knew how desperate I was. They knew that I couldn't take the quarantine anymore. Suddenly, my father walked up to me and hugged me. I didn't know how to feel about this because my father really hasn't ever acted this way. He looked up and I saw tears in his eyes too.

"Mijo," he replied with a broken voice. "I know you can't take much more of this. I can't tell you how difficult it is for me to see you change in such a negative way. Trust me that I don't want to do this to you on purpose. For now, just wait because it is still too dangerous outside."

I was shocked. All I could do is wait until the situation in New Jersey got better. The worst part of it is that video games started to bore me and the calls with my girlfriend started to not feel the same as if we were seeing each other face to face. What really broke my heart was when she called me once and burst into tears.

"Albert," she said. "With all my heart I miss you. Please come back to me."

Some words she said I was unable to understand because she was crying while she was talking. We were having an argument.

Some arguments you win, and some you lose. Some you win for the wrong reasons. And some you lose even though you did everything right. Some arguments you don't want to win even while you are fighting to do so. And some arguments you can't lose.

I just wish we could all stop fighting.

Thirty-Five

By Ashley Valerio

I've heard stories of people who go crazy on lock-down. For me, it took less than a week of quarantine before I started killing. Soon, I was murdering with abandon, killing millions just for the fun. I took glee in ending lives. I was out to end germs, and I would do it if I had to destroy them one by one.

When I would have to go out to the grocery store with my parents or just to get some fresh air, I was overwhelmed by the thought that there were germs everywhere: life ending, rapidly evolving germs. I knew they inhabited almost every nook and cranny of the Earth's surface. And for the very first time, I was scared.

As Corona rampaged around the globe, news outlets said to be very cautious because the virus could be on any surface. They repeated that those who are infected could transmit it through the air. I did not need to be told twice. In my eyes, every surface was infected, every particle of air a potential hazard, every walk through my house a journey through No Man's Land.

Today, I make sure to kill as many germs as possible. I wash my hands after touching anything, clean my phone and laptop with Clorox Wipes, take a shower as soon as I get home and remove my shoes off before entering my house.

I am a killer, and I have no remorse or guilt. I will kill again.

Thirty-Six

By Madissen Aligo

A week or two before we learned the school shut down, I had been told that I would be having knee surgery for an injury that happened in October. Instead of having my muscles around my patella strengthen so my kneecap wouldn't pop out again, I had been pushing for the surgery. Before the surgery I had been adjusting well to the online schooling. When I had come home I was feeling good, and wasn't feeling any pain. The days after the surgery, however, were hell; my knee felt like it was on fire anytime I moved and I was so uncomfortable. I didn't leave my bed unless it was to go use the bathroom and felt trapped in my own body. Knowing that I couldn't walk or leave my house felt so suffocating.

I hate not having control of things, especially myself. After the pain was gone and I was comfortable again, but I was unmotivated to get up and do any work. I felt that school was just a waste of time, knowing that none of it was in our control just made me want to give up. As I grew unmotivated to continue school, I grew unmotivated to continue working on my knee therapy as well.

At night, I sometimes stay awake and wonder what it would take to be motivated again.

Thirty-Seven

By Era Lushaj

Senior year was something I truly looked forward to. All the movies and TV shows I had ever seen about it told me this was going to be the best year of my life. Watching my older brother and cousins live out their final year of high school through celebrations, made me excited for when it would eventually be my turn.

I personally never liked high school, and couldn't wait to get out, especially after junior year. Junior year of high school was my most difficult and stressful school year, and I wanted nothing more than for it to be over. When it was finally over, I pushed myself to make the best of my senior year. After overcoming countless requirements and getting everything done accurately and on time, I was ready to experience senior year in the best way possible.

As much as I sympathize with those affected by the virus, I think that I am allowed to be sad about missing out on the best part of senior year. Granted the pandemic is very grave, and I personally know people close to me who have suffered its consequences, but I was just starting to relax and enjoy my final moments of high school. It sounds selfish to complain over something like this, but it really took a toll on me and my mental health as well.

I miss my friends. I miss being able to socialize outside in public places. As summer is nearing, I am very upset that I can't go on spontaneous trips with my friends and make memories before we all go off to college. The way things are going I don't believe we will have a normal summer. It truly hurts to say that I won't get the chance to walk across the stage, or experience prom like so many before me have done.

The world may be awful, but I'm still allowed to be sad.

Thirty-Eight

By Albin Lopez

It was the best senior year ever. For starters, this year I finally got to experience prom. I rented a nice house with a pool down by the shore. It was a great place to party! At night, my friends and I walked the boardwalk, and hung out on the balcony listening to music. The late spring weather was amazing.

The prom though, was only the start. After so many summers studying and readying myself for the "next" year, I finally had a chance to take a breather before college. I was able to reunite with my best friends and cousins. Together, we went to state parks like Bear Mountain. We had barbecues. One time, we wound up at Great Adventure and rode all the rides twice. Now that I was 18, I was also able to go to a music festival: The Electric Zoo in New York. What a night! What a summer! What an adventure!

I wish you could have seen it.

I wish I could have too.

Thirty-Nine

By Damion Salinas

Envy is a beast that lives within us, I've heard people say. Today, I envy those who continue to live their lives without worry. I envy the fact that they don't have to or choose not to worry about contracting this virus the way I do. I envy those with the luxury of going outside when they want, to do the things they want to do. I envy those who go outside without masks and gloves, even though I think they shouldn't. I envy those who are able to be home without being drained. I envy those who aren't driven crazy by the people they live with. I envy those who don't have to lock themselves in the room. I envy those whose schedules aren't ruined, who don't see the sunrise from their windows. I envy students who have their prom, who walk across the stage for graduation. I envy those who don't have to finish high school through a computer screen.

Envy is a beast who lives within us, I've heard people say. It is the only beast I feed.

Forty

By Neda Razmjou

The choices we make affect the world around us. Don't believe me? Just look at how the world around us has been and will be for a long time. I never truly grasped the concept of choice and change. I understood how it worked, but never thought it could be tied into something so big. Clearly, I was very wrong because choice and change is what this whole pandemic is associated with.

What is the biggest lesson that I have learned during this experience of social distancing and quarantine? I learned just how selfish people will always be, no matter what the circumstances are. I constantly see people gathering in large groups, people I even call friends, hanging out every day, going into public and possibly spreading the virus. They have no clue what impact they are putting on society, how many people they may have been responsible for killing, just because they wanted to hang out with friends. They may have impacted a stranger's life by being the cause of their loved one dying. With all the different forms of social media, there is no excuse as to why people can't just call their friends during these times. It's the most selfish thing one can do, and it really destroyed my faith in humanity.

The choices we make affect the world around us. Don't believe me? Just look at how the world around us has been and will be for a long time. I never truly grasped the concept of choice and change. I understood how it worked, but never thought it could be tied into something so big.

I'll never understand the choice to be selfish.

Forty-One

By Selin Askin

Every day I wake up terrified. Coronavirus terrifies me. Living where I do terrifies me. I hear stories of people dying and watch the number of cases go up live, which terrifies me. I do not know how to speak up and tell my parents because I do not want to stress them out. I do not know what to do with all this fear.

The last few months of senior year are supposed to be the best months of your life. Instead, I have spent these months at home, sleeping my life away to escape the fear.

When my parents first came to America, they left more than just Turkey; they left their families. My parents promised themselves that I would grow up knowing not only the place they came from but the people we came from as well. Going every summer has become such an important time for me because I can learn more about the history of the people and place my parents proudly call home. But with everything going on, I cannot go back and reconnect with them. I was looking forward to spending time with my uncle, who is unfortunately suffering from kidney failure, for what may be the last time. I fear that I will never be able to see him again. One of my fondest memories of my uncle is him taking me horseback riding. Being so young I was scared, but he taught me that I would be okay and that he would be there.

Who do I turn to now to tell me everything will be ok?

Forty-Two

By Arianna Khelil

I

Some weeks ago, my dad experienced chest pain, which necessitated a 911 call. I was afraid, and I didn't know what to do to comfort my family. As the pandemic raged unabated, we were told that we shouldn't be around others or invite them into our home. "Is it safe for my family and I to allow total strangers, all on the frontline, to come into our home to help my dad?" My mind raced. Soon, the EMS came geared with masks and gloves, and provided my dad with the help he needed before taking him to the hospital. "Will he be safe getting treatment among so many COVID patients?" I was very scared but left only to trust in the kindness of strangers. I hoped my father knew how much I loved him.

II

My dad needed continuous care due to cardiac issues. At Hackensack University Hospital, my dad had had a stent put into his heart, which would alleviate the chest pain he was experiencing. When this didn't work, my family decided to go to Mount Sinai Hospital to see a specialist in Brachytherapy. My head was spinning. The concern over COVID became secondary to me. "Would this finally be the answer to help my dad feel better?" I would've never imagined my first time driving over the George Washington Bridge was to take my dad to Mount Sinai Hospital. When we got there, we were not allowed in. My father would have to take this on his own. We kissed my dad goodbye and went home to await the news.

III

The brachytherapy procedure was successful. I was happy to see a huge smile on my dad's face, coming up the stairs as my dog, Reeses, was waiting for him at the top. This was one of the first times I've seen my dad come up the stairs without any chest pain. "Did the brachytherapy really work?" Right out of the hospital, my dad went to BJ's Wholesale Club to get food for dinner. "Typical dad," I thought. He was back to cooking a full course meal for us and cleaning the house. He is strong, so seeing him do what he loves reassured me he had felt better. I was hopeful my dad would finally get a good night's rest, with no chest pain to wake him.

Our hopes were soon crushed. The chest pain was back. My dad called out for me in the middle of the night. He was pale and sweaty. In a panic, I woke up my mom. I felt a tremendous guilt, which permeated me for all the times I was not the nicest to my dad. He cried and apologized to me, something I have never seen him do before. I told him there was no need to apologize, but I knew he just didn't want me to see him in pain. My heart broke to see a strong man, the pillar of our family, break down. The next day, the cardiologist explained this happens in a small percentage of people who get brachytherapy. "Why couldn't he win the lottery instead?" I pondered. He would require stenting once more.

IV

As I write this, the doctor called to inform me that a catherization shows my father's problem is not the artery they had fixed: It is other arteries which require bypass, possibly quadruple bypass. I feel hopeless. We cannot be at the hospital. Not only am I not by my dad's side, I didn't even get the chance to wish him luck before his surgery. I think about my dad and what must be going through his mind. We are praying to God to guide the surgeon's hands. We are praying to God to have my dad come out of this surgery safely and better than before.

By the time you read this, we will know how his surgery played out. We will know whether he lived or died.

Send word. Tell me my dad *knows* how loved he is.

Forty-Three

By Natalie Garay

As a few weeks of home instruction turned into months, the more I realized I would be looking back on my senior year differently than any other generation. It was easy at first to not think about the COVID-19 pandemic because everyone seemed so optimistic. But as the weeks of quarantine and death continued, it was hard to stay positive. For me and many others, we were left only to confront the feeling of loss: loss of love, loss of people, loss of time and, in more selfish ways, loss of prom and graduation. I would not get to feel the happiness of normal. Instead, I will look back to a time when I could only walk into my house if I drenched myself in disinfectant.

I think the only positive of this pandemic is understanding that loss doesn't have to be final. We all lose things, and sometimes, we find the lost thing and everything is ok again. And, sometimes, we find something even better.

This is it now. This is history. This is the new normal.

But, in the end, it's only one chapter.

The stories, our stories, will continue.

VOLUME II

Second Wave

One

By Sofia Martinez

Seven months have passed, and I've become almost numb to the "unprecedented" series of events the pandemic has brought. I'm less surprised by the bad things now. If anything, I think I should be angry. Angry that it has come to this. Angry that so many people were unable to put aside their own selfishness and properly quarantine for the sake of the whole. But then again, the anger wouldn't fix things. I'm tired more than anything. Lately, I've just been grateful for my family's health and for the safety of my loved ones.

***

Oddly enough, I can't shake the feeling that everything feels so fake. Reality feels distorted. I feel almost detached from it. It's like I'm living in a movie, or a video game, if that makes more sense - one of those dystopian films where a plague breaks out and the world falls to shambles as the people all scramble to protect themselves. And the directors have really put in all the little details to sell it. On set they have tons of signs that read "Do your part! Stay 6 ft apart!" and big billboards advertising masks in the background of many scenes, just in case you forgot what kind of movie this is. When the characters are out, maybe grocery shopping, a monotone voice will boom from the speakers with a reminder to "please remember to keep a safe distance from all customers! Have a nice day!" And maybe they'll include some wide shots of the empty streets too and the masks littered on the floor, flying about with the wind, or the news reports on the TVs monitoring death tolls. Ah yes, they've gathered all the little details for their setting, now it *really* screams "pandemic," To the audience, this is just a fake world the directors created. "Just imagine what living like *that* would be like", they could think to themselves - safe and content with their normal lives.

Unfortunately, the virus outbreak is not the plot of a movie and will not go away from our lives with some long list of end credits. We can't turn off the screen. We can't just watch a happier movie. The virus is just the sick and twisted reality we happen to endure.

Amidst all this, I want to stay hopeful for a solution. I really do. Yet since the beginning it's been nothing but empty promises for a return to normalcy. We thought we'd be quarantined for two weeks. Then, no, three. No, a month. No, just until the summer for sure. No. Wrong again. It's gone on for too long. And just taking things day by day is not much comfort anymore. Everyone said to keep a routine for your sanity, but it's the *repetitiveness* of the days themselves that becomes unsettling. You can't expect much to change when you're confined mostly to home. At some point, every day begins to feel the same. At some point, you find yourself dazed by the never-ending cycle of it. At some point, the days blend into weeks, blend into months, and finally blend into a tedious loop where you're reliving the same day as yesterday. And the day before that. And the day before that. And...

***

Seven months have passed, and I've become almost numb to the "unprecedented" series of events the pandemic has brought. I'm less surprised by the bad things now. If anything, I think I should be angry. Angry that it has come to this. Angry that so many people were unable to put aside their own selfishness and properly quarantine for the sake of the whole. But then again, the anger wouldn't fix things. I'm tired more than anything. Lately, I've just been grateful for my family's health and for the safety of my loved ones.

Two

By Wilbert Roca Alvarez

Who gives you help when no one can help? What happens when you need care, but no one can care for you or themselves?

Normally, when a person gets infected by COVID-19 they would be made to self-quarantine in their rooms and be helped by their friends or relatives. They would be cared for, distancing themselves from others, wearing masks and gloves, and the family would disinfect everything and clean, clean, clean. However, my whole family caught COVID-19 at the same time. Six of us, sick together, with only the sickness of others to keep us company.

I was the first. As the plague raged outside, I kept hearing stories of people getting sick. I feared for my safety as it spread like wildfire. One day not long after I woke up with my body drained of energy - like my chest was held down by weights. I was hot like a furnace. I thought it must be the common cold since there was no way I got COVID. A week later my father was very ill himself, and suffered from fatigue, headaches, and a fever. My half-brother would end up taking him to the doctor to see if he had Corona and returned with medicine and an inhaler of some sort. He was the second.

Two days later, we all went to a testing facility. My older sister had to drive, as my parents couldn't. I felt like we were experiments when they swabbed our noses and took samples. My father's body was aching, and he was vomiting in bags on the way there. I hoped they got to us soon since my dad was getting worse and worse: He couldn't move out of bed, didn't want to eat, and had diarrhea.

We decided to let my dad sleep in a room by himself. We made my mom sleep on the couch. I would cook and clean the house while both of them would spend most of their days resting. Both of their fevers continued to get worse. A week later we got the results. We were all positive for COVID.

And then there were none.

A sudden realization hit me: what were we going to do about the upcoming rent, about the food and supplies we needed? We couldn't go out. My parents couldn't work anymore, and a stimulus check wouldn't be given out until much later - even then, it wouldn't be enough.

I was distressed. My two younger sisters were already starting to lose their taste and smell. They couldn't really help us out with certain things, and I didn't want them to go out at all. I didn't want to let them down.

We did what we could on our own, including home medications we could devise. I helped my mother set up a vaporizer of sorts with eucalyptus, chamomile, lemon, ginger, and coffee all mixed together in a big pot and heated. This would make very hot steam and you could put your face in the mixture. I did this several times and it cleared my nostrils. I felt like I could actually breath.

All we could do wasn't enough. My mother was having sharp pains in her chest and trouble breathing. As scared as we were to go out, I was more terrified of my mother dying in our house, especially if there was something I could do. I decided to call a nearby hospital in order to ask them for assistance. They asked me what her condition was and if it was COVID related. Even with a positive test they told me on the phone that they were too backed-up, and that my mother's symptoms were not severe enough to admit her.

There was truly no one left to care for us when we needed care the most. Eventually, me and my older sister, who was recovering quicker, would drive to get supplies. We still hadn't gotten a negative test which would have cleared us, but we had to do what we could or else go hungry. We put on two facemasks and all kinds of protective gear. Somewhere in there, my sister herself infected her boyfriend, who she only saw when we went shopping. I still wonder and feel guilty about the possibility we infected someone else at the supermarket. Hunger allowed no choice. Those who face indifference must sometimes be indifferent in return.

As weeks passed, we all eventually felt better. Grateful to be alive, and seemingly well, the emotion we most felt was gratitude. On a whim, we decided to make tamales and delivery to my cousin's porch. He had brought food once. And that helped. My cousin refused our food - our food we had fought so hard to get and which we now offered to share with him. He was scared the tamales could infect him and get him sick. This same cousin is soon entering military training. This does not scare him. His own family does.

I wonder if he will come back scared and feeling like there is nobody to care for him. I wonder if he will be rebuffed, as so many veterans are, from the support and the care they need. I wonder if, one day, he will feel abandoned and alone.

I wonder if he knows that, when the world turns its back on him, that I will be there - that the best we can do is care for each other.

Three

By Zena Hassan

It was in the middle of plague quarantine that my father decided we were short on basic necessities. Since I had been stuck at home as well, I asked to tag along with him to our local Walmart. I placed my mask on. As we walked inside the store, I noticed that there was a sense of unease within each person - their movement away from each other, their fear of being too close to somebody else - an uneasiness that manifested as distance, making tangible the anxiety we all felt inside. Walking to the cereal aisle, I passed a middle-aged man walking opposite me, two aisles down where I was. This man started to cough uncontrollably, in a way that was concerning. The sound of the wheels of shopping carts increased as the people hurried away. Nobody looked. Nobody helped. Looks of disgust and horror froze on peoples' faces, their sympathy evaporated in desperate hopes for their own survival.

Fleeing myself, I looked back as I turned the last corner. The man was still there. He had fallen to the ground. He was still coughing. Alone.

Four

By Carla Paz-Almonte

For as long as I could remember, my grandmother lived in a nursing home. This was supposed to protect her since she had dementia. Until it didn't. Her nursing home was one of the ones hit hard by COVID and she was diagnosed with the disease soon after. Many of the nurses and other patients staying there got sick and died. When my dad got the call, I tried to comfort him but he wanted to be left alone. In the following week, my dad tried to visit her in the hospital. The nurses didn't let him in because of the obvious risk. He pleaded, but my dad knew it was for the best.

Soon after, the hospital called to tell us that my grandmother had died. When my dad said the words, "My mom is dead?" the entire house went silent. I looked at my sister and her eyes were glistening. I quickly got up and locked myself in the bathroom so

I could cry. When I came back into my room, my mom was there comforting my sister. When I saw my mom, I broke into tears again. I cried in her arms for a few minutes. I wanted to avoid seeing my dad for as long as possible since I knew I would cry once I saw him. We went downstairs and to my surprise, I did not bawl my eyes out right away. We tried to talk to him, but he was on the phone with family members to tell them the news. My sister and I went upstairs and tried to go to sleep.

I could barely sleep that night because of everything that happened. I could barely sleep for nights afterwards. The thought of losing my family members and everyone I cared about kept me up at night. I thought about all the memories I have of my grandmother, visiting her at the nursing home. I wondered if, because of her dementia she remembered me. For most of these nights, I cried myself to sleep.

The only person who attended my grandmother's funeral was my dad. The rest of the family could not go because we were all scared of getting the virus. My dad came back and wanted to be left alone for the rest of the day. He wanted to be alone because he could have been exposed to the virus and because of his own grief. All I wanted to do was try to comfort him, but I couldn't.

For months afterwards, the thought of losing my family invaded my thoughts. I kept thinking about how broken I would be. Did my grandma know what was happening? Did she understand that she was suffering with a virus that could possibly kill her? Did she still think she was in El Salvador? Was memory a blessing? Or a curse?

I isolated myself from my friends and my sister for months because I did not want to tell them what I was going through. Sometimes they would mention that they miss me. I, too, was becoming just a memory.

Eventually, my friends confronted me saying that I was barely there and that it was affecting our relationship. I tried to play it off as me wanting some alone time and not needing someone there for me, but they were right. I felt horrible about not being there for them when they were always there for. But I didn't want to tell them about my internal struggle.

I finally decided that I had to open up to someone about how I've been feeling so I went to my sister. I told her everything I was feeling and how scared I was to lose everyone I care about. She comforted me, telling me everyone will die eventually but we don't have to worry about it now. My grandma did not suffer and died peacefully. In my mind, I knew that she did not know what was going on. This brought me comfort. I think knowing that you are dying makes the end even worse - the memory of what was scaring you into not letting go.

One night, I tell myself, she went to bed for the last time. And just before the end, she suddenly remembered. And it wasn't sad. She closed her eyes, my grandmother, and she dreamt of El Salvador. She dreamt of her two kids. She dreamt of me.

Five

By Jorge Urias

My family wanted to surprise my grandpa for his birthday. He wasn't expecting anything special, nothing more of a phone call to say the least. Their street was a dead-end, so not a lot of cars would pass by, making it the perfect place for an outdoor party. We bought stuff like balloons, horns, and even a banner to make sure this would be something to remember. The day of his birthday, my family met up by my grandparents' house to set up. As he came down the street, we hid behind cars. My heart was beating fast from the excitement, I haven't had fun like this in a long time. Just when he was right across the street, we jumped out and waved the banner at him. My grandpa was so surprised. I don't think he knew what to do. He beeped the car at us and waved out the window. My grandma was laughing beside him and waving at everyone; playing along like she didn't know what was happening. Once they parked the car and came out, everyone went to my grandpa to greet him.

We haven't gathered like this in a long time, so for everyone to be there together felt just like old times. We couldn't hug or shake hands with my grandparents (which hurt me a little because I wanted to badly), so we used the newest trend: elbow greetings. After being acquainted with each other and getting over the whole surprise, everyone went into full family mode.

It was like a switch had turned on. Everyone started to talk about how everything had been and what we all do at home. Conversations about food and sports occurred left and right. It was hard to even hear yourself. There were about 9 of us all together (just under the gathering limit), but everyone was still on edge, worried we would get in trouble. Having to keep your mask on while talking (especially with glasses on) and not having physical contact was hard, but for that one moment, everything felt normal. For that one brief moment, everybody was laughing. Everybody was happy. Nobody was indoors or next to a computer. We were together, and the Coronavirus did not exist.

Six

By Winnie Zhao

I was weak.

I didn't know how, but I got COVID-19. I felt sick, but more than that, I felt guilty, and ashamed, and alone.

I remember the day before my COVID-19 symptoms started to show, I had a family gathering and was OK. The very next day I felt paralyzed. That was when my days of agony and torture started. I was coughing, feverish, and tired. I know for a fact that I am a healthy teenager and to be so feeble and weak was very unlike me. At the time, I didn't know all of the symptoms of COVID-19. Looking back, I know now I should have literally isolated myself from everyone, but I stayed in my room with my sister. Because COVID-19 was so new, I didn't know how to ask for the help I needed most. My family left me alone in the house, and I kept my vulnerabilities private. It was only after my mom got home from work that she knew something was wrong. She seemed to know what to do. First, she separated me into another room upstairs near hers, so she could keep a close eye on me. Testing at the time was limited and hard to get, so we were left wondering whether COVID-19 was even the culprit. Somehow, I was able to get tested. I was positive.

I was *weak*.

At first, I was full of anger for somehow contracting the virus, then it was the worries about what would happen next. *Would my condition get better or worse? Had I infected my sister? Would I be a burden?* All of these thoughts rushed into my head at once. I was panicking. My mom was there to take care of me. but as a few days passed, my mom started to cough and develop a high fever too. At this point, neither of us were able to do much. But my mom still worried about me. She would come into my room, while she herself was in as much pain as I was and pour me ginger tea. Even breathing was hard. Every night I thought about how she did it. I felt that I was responsible for her weak state.

Because I was weak.

Soon my condition got to the point where my sense of smell and taste were absent. I didn't want to tell my mom that I couldn't smell or taste anymore because I thought that it would stress her even more.

I kept it to myself. I thought that my condition was only going to get worse. As a result, I started to bathe myself in information about COVID-19, but I needed someone or something to reassure me that everything would be OK. I looked to stories about others who had COVID-19 and even videos on Youtube about their experiences. Looking back now, it was a terrible idea to engulf myself on the internet. I started to see the increased numbers of deaths and I thought to myself if I was going to be part of it. I brought only more fear to myself and to my mom. While I was upstairs by myself, I thought about a lot of things. My thoughts and feelings were everywhere. One moment I was jealous of my sister when I thought about my chances of surviving. At times I wondered if my condition from the first night would come back out of nowhere again.

I think it was about three weeks up in the room until I had fully recovered. Now, when I see someone outside, I avoid them. At some point, I stopped going to play tennis for fear of contracting the virus again. I can't even go back to the room where I was in - all those long, lonely nights. I think about the pain I went through. Sometimes, because of trauma, I feel I am still in that pain today. I was weak.

I am weak still.

Seven

By Monalise Mucha

I didn't want to go to Connecticut that day. I wanted to stay home.

My parents asked me repeatedly, however, and soon, we were all in the car. It wasn't such a nice day, to be fair. It was cloudy. I don't particularly like going out on cloudy days.

I sat on the back seat of the car and listened to music the whole time. I looked out at the window and tried not to pay attention to my phone during the trip. After all, I've had enough of the internet. We left New Jersey, and the road continued empty and lifeless. "Imagine this for two more hours," I thought. I just stared out the window, at the car door, the roof, and anything else I could.

Soon, the road changed. Complete nothingness transformed into sprouting orange and red trees. They were so tall and so pretty. The sun wasn't bright, but that didn't matter. Fallen leaves had surrounded the road, coloring it and making it brighter. Beautiful leaves. *Dead leaves*.

Months go by so fast. I realize it's almost winter. Soon it will be Christmas Eve. And then New Year's. I think about all the time that disappeared right before my eyes, as if yesterday was September 2019, and I was in school with the people I knew.

Fall was also lovely then.

It still baffles me that it has been so long. As each day repeats itself, I begin to feel like the leaves, fallen since quarantine.

I'm tired. When will life be what it used to be?

The view from the car could have easily made me sad, but instead, this day, I felt nostalgic. Little things like the physical changes of nature, seeing someone we know across the street, or even passing by the store closest to your house can be extremely valuable to a person. They help us remember. They help us connect to the moments in our lives where we were the happiest.

The days are still nice. I've gotten to see my friends a few times. I've even made new friends. I've learned new things. I've gotten a chance to understand myself and people around me better. Maybe, I think, some days can be gray as long as there is even one full of color.

We arrived at our destination. We were visiting a family friend. Their house, too, was surrounded by scarlet trees. The sun came out a little bit now, its light melting through the leaves. It truly was a sight for sore eyes. We stayed until dark, watching the leaves fall.

Watching them, marveling at their change and the beauty they inspired, I began to wonder: when leaves fall do they too remember what it was like to be alive? What it was like to be green?

Eight

By Julianna Baldwin

If you have ever been on a roller coaster, then you know the worst part: the long, tortuous uphill battle to get over the first hill. While you sit on the ride, you hold your breath and hang on for dear life. You try to make yourself feel better and tell yourself that, "it's all going to be alright." On this painstakingly long uphill journey, you make predictions about what will happen when you get to the top of the hill. Even though you have seen what the ride looks like before, and you know there will be a huge drop, you are never truly prepared for what will happen when you round that edge. Every roller coaster has the same beginning; that same boring, scary ride up the first hill, followed by the same treacherous free fall.

For me, COVID-19 feels like the initial climb on the roller coaster. Every single day feels the exact same. Every day, I wake up just to do what? Nothing. Every day I go to bed, just to do what? Nothing tomorrow. If every day is just bleeding into the next, and there is no differentiation among the hours, then what is the point of doing anything? So what do I do? Nothing. I go to school but I am not really there, my mind is focused on calculating how many minutes I have left until I can crawl back into my bed. Everyone tells us, "it's going to be alright," but that isn't true. Everything has changed, and it will never go back to normal. I will never have the same motivation to go to school for the full seven hours or to do the same pointless assignments for homework. I will always be living in overwhelming terror and anxiety; the same terror and anxiety you feel on your way up those steep, intimidating roller coaster tracks.

I was never prepared for what COVID-19 would bring into my life. Just like we are never prepared for what we will endure as we round the first peak on the roller coaster. We have no idea what is going to happen because we can't see over the hump; we are constantly being blindsided and are expected to just roll with the punches. I take naps because when I close my eyes, I am transported to another world, a world I can control, somewhere I can make my own scenarios and escape the horror of this never-ending journey. On a roller coaster, you close your eyes to escape; to distract yourself from reality, to calm yourself down. I have no control over anything anymore. All decisions are made without me: sports, clubs, and opportunities being stripped from my hands. I close my eyes and am judged for wanting to take a nap.

There is no way to get away from COVID-19, just like there is no way to get off of the roller coaster. Once you are strapped in, and heading up those tracks, there is no turning back. I am stuck on this life- altering uphill battle with no motivation, no voice, and no escape. But "it's going to be alright," right?

Close your eyes. Raise your hands. Scream. What does it matter? "It's going to be alright."

WEEEEEEE!

Nine

By Nareg Kassardjian

Where do you go to find God in a world where God seems to have disappeared? It is seven months into plague quarantine, and the doors of Saints Vartanantz Armenian Apostolic Church are closed.

For years, many people have challenged my identity and questioned it. "Oh, you really go to Church every Sunday, who cares? It's just a Church and you can't even see God; how do you know he's real?" However, despite my growing connection and relationship to God, my world changed due to limitations imposed on us from COVID-19. I'd miss the time-tested, millennia old holy hymns, the greetings at the door, the kisses of peace, the chants of allegiance to God and his Trinity. Most importantly, I'd miss my friends, the schools, and the community.

Like many, my life was shaken, my routine was shattered, and my identity was smoldered in the fire of a harsh reality. I didn't understand. I didn't understand why this was happening. At church, I looked forward to exploring Armenian literature, to teaching the next generation about our rich history, to influencing lives, and to preserving our language. I'd look forward to removing and recreating the bulletin board multiple times according to holiday or season, and perhaps, most importantly of all, I looked forward to the possibility of teaching my own class. The harsh, heart-breaking reality took a while to set in. I realized that I would no longer be able to hear the laughter of children or their attempts at challenging tongue twisters. I'd never see the patience of teachers wearing thin. I'd never see the long, yet fast-moving lines during lunch. I'd never feel the ground erupt during recess, or the walls quiver in silence after shouting caused by a loud row. I'd never be able to live in my preferred present, and I became unsure of my future. But there is no future in the COVID present.

My identity was put to the test and the aggressors won. I'd no longer be surrounded by poems of nature on the walls or hear the fervor of patriotic verses to songs I thought deeply on during concerts at the same Church. I'd no longer have youth group meetings, in which I had hoped to make more friends and explore new relationships. No longer would I be able to look forward to summer camps and, in turn, a revival of a Sunday school which once boasted 120 students.

Many people look at churches as an old-world concept, an idea foreign to a world growing far from traditional values and beliefs. However, this couldn't be further from my truth. My life was centered around my Church and the future I've pondered there became increasingly real to me. The resonating hymns heal my soul and relieve me from the stress of my teenage years and the burden of my ancestors. The burden I carry isn't a simple one. I owe it to my massacred family to preserve our shared language, religion, unwavering spirit, and pride. Truly, I tell you that my world did stereotypically 'turn upside down' and the pillars which held the foundations of my identity were shaken, only to collapse.

So, after all this, one important question remains unanswered: where is God? Has he left us, and why? The truth isn't easy to explain because we cannot find or understand God. However, maybe instead we can find signs of his creation and work sprinkled among us. His creation is in the animals we eat and the flowers we smell. His work is in the friends we make and the lessons we learn. His vengeance are the floods and earthquakes and, yes, plagues, that cause our feet to tremble.

Maybe God hasn't left, he's simply watching his creation. If God had truly left us, why does the sun still shine and why does the moon still beam? Why do the birds migrate and why do the salmon continue upstream? Our own lives and the precious lives of those around us have a purpose. How do we know our actions won't change the course of our human history? Maybe God hasn't left us. Perhaps he's just waiting to see what we will do.

The world outside makes it seem like God is closed. But we are still here. Still ready. Still open.

Ten

By Andrea I. Aguirre

At the beginning of September, I was talking to my best friend about random things as always: food, movies, daily activities, stress from homework. In retrospect, it was all just small talk to avoid addressing the bigger issues. A few minutes later I got a message:

"Andrea, please pray for my daddy," she wrote.

The first thing that came to mind was that something bad had happened. She told me that an ambulance had taken her father to the hospital because he was seriously ill, that it was difficult for him to breathe and that they believed it was Coronavirus. My mind went blank. I didn't know what to say. The only thing I got out was "Don't worry. Everything will be fine." She didn't answer. I knew she was crying, and I wanted to do something to help her, but I couldn't.

The days passed and we tried to continue talking normally, but of course it was not the same because of her father, who at this point had tested positive for COVID. When my friend was told the news, she was devastated, so devastated that she ended up getting sick. I wanted to be there for her and to give her a hug and to comfort her, but I couldn't.

I sent my friend messages constantly, saying that God was in control and not to worry and that her father would get better. But a call or a message doesn't mean the same thing as seeing someone in person does. Of course, regulations and good behavior prevented me from being with her in person, no matter how much I wanted to be. I felt helpless, and like I was failing our friendship. I wanted to be there for her in a place where words didn't matter, but I couldn't.

Weeks passed and her father did not get better. I felt more and more desperate given my inability to do anything. After a month, my friend's father finally left the hospital. I was very happy for her and her dad. I felt great relief knowing that everything was OK. But the feeling of being a failure and a terrible friend for not being there did not disappear. I wasn't there when my best friend needed me the most.

I wanted to write that this has made us all better. But I couldn't.

Eleven

By Angy El-Dakkak

My sister, Samera, lives in Syria with her husband and child, and owns her own pharmacy all at 26. Even though we live apart, she is everything to me, and I could never imagine my life without her in it. Growing up, she was more of a mother to me than my own mother was.

My whole family resides in and is originally from Damascus, Syria. I was also born there and lived there for a while. Syria is an extremely poor country with a horrendous healthcare system due, in large part, to an ongoing civil war. When Coronavirus started spreading, it was correctly predicted that if it were to get to the Middle East, struggling countries would be doomed. In Syria, there are army soldiers at every corner, electricity turns off every three hours, and hot water doesn't exist for many. All go to sleep in fear of not waking up because of the bombs and strikes that shake the windows and doors. Because there is not enough money to keep hospitals open, civilians mainly rely on medicines from pharmacies instead of hospitals and offices.

When COVID did end up hitting Syria, an extremely strict lockdown was put into effect. Nobody was allowed to go out after certain hours or they would be fined. Only pharmacies, like my sister's, could remain open. My family here made sure we always checked in on our family there. And for a long time they were fine until everything started opening up again. The president of Syria downplayed the virus, said everything was under control, told the people they were rounding the corner. Instinctively, my sister was excited that she could finally go out, and so she did. Soon, she herself caught Corona. She had been feeling extremely off. Testing in Syria is severely limited, but my sister, given her job, was able to get what she needed. When my mom said the words out loud, "Your sister has Coronavirus," everything just stopped: what I was doing, what I was thinking, I even lost my breath for a second out of shock.

I called my sister multiple times, but I had forgotten about the time difference. Once I knew she was up, I talked to her frequently. I did not want to show it, but my heart was shattering as I heard her struggling to make words. She would also send me pictures of her lying in bed, her nose and eyes all puffy. Every nerve in my body was terrified for her. Every time I texted her and she would take longer than ten minutes to respond, I could not control the awful thoughts in my mind. Samera was smart and quarantined for 2 weeks away from her husband and son. She got better. I thank God though because since she is a pharmacist, she was able to easily get the drugs she knew she needed. I have never been more relieved than when I found out she got better.

But could you imagine? Could you imagine living in a country where many of its people lived in fear, where half the country was at war with the other half? Where the president said that the virus was no big deal? Where testing was only available to certain people? Where only people with the right connections could get the medicine they needed? Where the sick were forced to be alone? And where even the very smartest and youngest and bravest could do nothing but hope and pray?

Thank God we live in America.

Twelve

By Megan Forro

With fewer and fewer places to go outside, the world online has become the only safe space left. That's how I met my new best friend.

I met him in a TikTok comment section in June. We added each other on Snapchat and had an instant connection that I had never had with anyone else before. Our conversations then and now are continuous, never dry, and bring a smile to my face every single day.

It feels as though we've known each other for years when, in reality, we don't even know each other at all.

We talked a lot on Snapchat, sending videos to each other. There was absolutely no awkward tension, which is quite rare for new friendships. We then exchanged phone numbers and began to talk on Facetime. We also exchanged Instagrams and continued to converse every single day. As the summer months went on, we grew closer and closer. He always helps cheer me on and encourages me when I get upset about things, no matter how miniscule the issue may be.

Despite the physical distance between us, we could not be any closer on an emotional level.

I hope to meet him as soon as possible. I hope he's as awesome in person as he is online. I hope the world changes, and travel is permissible, and I hope we can spend a day together in the sun.

Through quarantine and plague, because of him I hope at all.

Thirteen

By Dunia Darwich

When the forms for my school came out asking whether we wanted to be all-remote or hybrid for the upcoming year I knew my decision straight away. I went to my parents and showed them the form and said, "I want to be all-remote." My parents were relieved that I didn't want to be hybrid as they were worried about the spread of the virus. Our area had been particularly hard hit in the initial wave of the plague. We lost teachers at our school. Many people lost family members.

I wasn't willing to play Russian Roulette with that fear.

When the school year started, I received loads and loads of schoolwork. I was shocked and would often be working on homework from the minute school was done to around midnight. This equates to around eight-ten hours of schoolwork a day! A lot of this, I think, comes from constant changes in scheduling, and many teachers struggling in that paradigm to properly gauge workloads. Some of it probably also comes from the stop and start nature of the in-person learning - as we meet less and less, more and more is expected of us each time we do. It's exhausting.

On top of the increased workloads, remote learning has been quite a challenge. That's because I am a visual learner. As weird as it sounds, I learn from the teacher's hand and body movements. It's the most efficient way for me to learn. When you're at home, however, you can't see your teacher's body language. I've had to kind of adapt to that.

For all the challenges of remote learning, I don't regret this decision at all. This entire time, I've never had to worry if I had the virus or not. I've never had to worry about whether or not I was giving it to someone else. I have been home this entire time: alone, working on what I had to work on, keeping myself and other people safe.

It can be hard looking at the selfishness of others to stay focused. In the end, my going remote doesn't seem to matter when my school still operates. As long as some people are there, the community is still at risk.

But maybe one person is alive today because of my decision. Maybe I am.

I may be on distance learning, but I'm keeping you close in my heart.

Fourteen

By Jana Khalil

What I am about to tell you is not something I am supposed to discuss with anyone. Keep it secret. Keep it safe.

You see, I grew up in a very traditional Middle Eastern household, where Arabic is always spoken, and Arab culture is strictly adhered to. One of the bedrocks of Arab culture is that mental health issues of any kind are not to be discussed - ever. This has always been hard for me to accept, but it has become exceptionally difficult during quarantine. I am normally a very anxious person, but I feel my anxiety has only worsened since the pandemic started.

My anxiety peaked on the first day of remote learning. School had just been shut down, and many places of work had gone virtual as well. However, my dad still had to go into work. I was already nervous about how online school would go and how difficult it would be to adjust. However, that anxiety was quickly overshadowed by the fear I had for my father. He is high-risk for COVID-19, and I really wished he could just work from home. Throughout the day, all I could think about was him. Did he remember a mask? Are his coworkers social distancing? Was his building sanitized prior to employees entering? My mind was spinning in a million different directions, and I began to cry uncontrollably. I really tried to stop, but the more I did, the more tears dropped down my cheeks.

There was no way I could distract myself from all the fear I was feeling. It became hard to breathe, my chest started tightening up, and I was getting really dizzy. It seemed as if my body was fighting against itself and I couldn't handle it. I started to shake. "What is wrong with me?" I thought to myself. How could I get my body out of self-destruct mode? I decided to close my eyes and try to take some deep breaths in an attempt to regain control over my body. After many deep breaths, I was finally able to bring my body back from the brink of chaos.

I realized my anxiety had never gone this far before, and I was concerned. But what was I going to do with this concern? Who could I tell? My family would either dismiss me completely if I told them or make me feel ashamed for even discussing such a thing. And so every day, my anxiety would only get worse. Every little thing would cause me to worry. If a family member were not in their room when I thought they would be, my mind would instantly think the worst, like they had caught COVID without me knowing and are being hospitalized.

I was constantly mentally exhausted.

I felt suffocated with all these thoughts and feelings, and I just wanted to let it all go. But I couldn't. There was no one to turn to. For Arabs, issues with mental health are an embarrassment, not only to the individual, but the entire family as well. I felt stuck. Arab culture is very strict, and if I were to ever try even to hint at any mental struggles, I would be shut down immediately. This stigma around mental health in my culture leaves no room to breathe. Instead, I keep everything to myself. I was never given the outlet to express how I feel, and now all those unreleased feelings are coming back to haunt me.

What I just told you is not something I am supposed to discuss with anyone. Keep it secret.

Keep me safe.

Fifteen

By Ata Erdal

"In a real dark night of the soul it is always three o'clock in the morning, day after day."
—*F. Scott Fitzgerald*

Many people have described the effects of COVID-19 as flipping their world upside-down. For me and my family, the long months of quarantine managed to do this literally.

While others have described quarantine as a shift in reality, the lonely days of plague shifted my sense of time. Before COVID-19 had forced us into our homes, my routine prioritized time management. Once the "stay-at-home" orders were put into effect, however, time did not feel important anymore. No one had to leave the house for school or work. Nobody had anywhere to be. At first, I was just staying up later at night, trying to make the best out of not having to get up extra early to get ready for school. Eventually, though, my sleep schedule became nearly nonexistent. Some days - weekends in particular - I would sleep during the day and be awake during the night.

This is how my family and I managed to celebrate my father's birthday at 3:00AM. That day, I woke up sometime between 8 and 9 PM. Yes, 9 o'clock at night. It was my father's birthday, and my whole family had slept through the entire day. This wasn't surprising to us at the time. We had been sleeping during the day quite often. Just as any regular day would begin, we proceeded to eat breakfast shortly after getting up. Lunch was at around midnight, dinner at around 2 AM. And of course, we had to celebrate my father's birthday with a beautiful cake. At 3:00 AM that morning, we lit the candles on the cake and ate. My father made a wish.

At 3 AM, my world flipped upside-down, but surrounded by those I loved the most, I wondered if he wished for morning to finally come.

Or perhaps, even in the middle of the night, it was here already.

Sixteen

By Sofia Loiacono

.

I feel like I'm in an old, jerky car travelling through the pandemic. Just as I begin to get comfortable with the flow of life, and the strange circumstances it presents, the car decides to break down with little warning and throw all of its passengers forward. I get whiplash.

But one constant outlet I've found during these tough times has been dancing. I've been dancing since I was two years old, so having to stop so suddenly in March was a revelation for me. For a couple of years, I'd been going through dance as if it were just another required activity, like school and homework. Having to stop dancing completely made me realize how much I actually love to dance and how unhappy my old studio had made me. It wasn't the dancing itself that made me unhappy, but the fact that I wasn't getting satisfaction from the people I was surrounded by. Through these past months with a new studio, I've been able to dedicate more of my time to my passion for dance, and I've been able to accomplish more than I have in the past seven years of competitive dancing combined.

This year, I was given my second ever solo. My first solo was given to me last year, during my junior year of high school, but, because of the virus, I couldn't compete or perform. Last year I was devastated because I thought I was too old to be starting solos.

Typically, in the dance world, the younger you start out, the better off you are. It's not unheard of, but it's unusual for a sixteen- or seventeen-year-old to be getting their first solo ever, let alone an almost eighteen-year-old like me. In the past three months of practicing, I worked hard with incredible choreographers who put the time into wearing masks during a global pandemic and were still coming to teach students. They put in so much work to make sure that we were safe, and that business could continue as usual. Because of their dedication, I have a beautiful dance that I get to show off to my parents, my peers, and the dance world.

I also competed for the first time in almost a year during this pandemic, and it's fascinating how different everything is and how much work goes into making sure that the dance world can continue. For example, there are only two studios allowed in the building at a time, as opposed to the maybe twenty that would be together during a normal season. Only seven parents, as well as our coaches, are allowed in the building at that time, where we are given our own space to practice, warm up, and perform. In a typical season, the venue is packed full of dancers, parents, and audience members, and it's difficult to even move around. It was strange being in such an empty building.

It's also incredibly different not being able to see the faces of our parents, our families, and our peers in the crowd cheering us on, all wearing our studio colors of bright green. However, the competition live-streamed our performance so everybody could see it. While I couldn't see everybody I knew supporting me, I know that they were there through a screen cheering me on. Just the fact that my family and friends wanted to see my performance enough that they figured out the live-streaming platform warms my heart.

For me, the biggest positive to such a terrible pandemic is the bonds formed between my team members and me. It's difficult doing a team sport that relies on such trust between people to stay six feet apart. It's hard to imagine doing this kind of team sport physically apart, but the bond that we've created between us is incredible.

It's a wonderful feeling having a whole group of people who have gone through and are going through the same thing. But it isn't all positive. We're disappointed every week because of big and small differences. Our Thanksgiving party, for example, was, of course, cancelled. This would have been my first, and only, chance to experience this event.

The virus made me realize how incredibly lucky I am to be in a place where I have such easy access to my passions. I was able to find a studio that I loved and coaches who gave me their full support within a short span of time, and I know that not a lot of people have that opportunity. I would never have left the space I was in if it weren't for the shutdown.

In the end, sometimes, even the jankiest of cars brings you where you need to go.

Seventeen

By Rubi Orellana

COVID-19 brought me to a deep and dark place I never wanted to reach.

I lost motivation to do anything. I completely lacked self-love. I judged every part of me. It made me angry that I felt like this. I was disgusted when I looked at myself in the mirror. I couldn't look without tearing up.

It is tiring to always feel like I need to look a certain way to feel "beautiful."

Starting to move around was hard. Little steps lead to bigger ones. I started by working out: Ten minutes every two weeks. That was a challenge to me. I did the workouts without caring. Sometimes, I even cried and had to stop.

I knew I could not force myself to continue.

Lacking the ability to self-motivate, I began surrounding myself with people that motivated me.

I have a very supportive family. They helped me be a better person. I walked with my family and did my personal workouts. I did the things I loved. I focused on playing the piano. I played more tennis. I tried cooking, learned how to make bracelets, and even learned how to paint. I became more passionate about singing. I started to really open up. I did the things I loved. I tried new things.

Everyone can have a bad day. Sometimes there will be darkness but all of us can beat that darkness. I beat it. All I had to do was have a little faith in myself that I will be a better me.

COVID-19 brought me to a deep and dark place I never wanted to reach.

I will never reach that place again.

Eighteen

By Anela Deljanin

Dear Hazyza,

You're probably not even going to read this. You won't listen even if you do.

Going into quarantine there was a vague hope that, forced to be around the same people for months on end, families would grow tighter. I suppose when you spend so much time with the same people, one of two things can happen; you can end up loving the person so much more or end up hating them worse. I'm not sure what is the case with us.

For years, the relationship we had with each other was the type of relationship people wished for. Everyone would always tell me how badly they wanted the relationship we had with each other. We would both confide in each other and tell each other things that we would never even think to tell Saida or Mama. We were always attached to each other like skin and bone.

We spent every waking moment after school on my bed either watching shows and talking to each other, or simply on our phones just enjoying the others' presence. But it wasn't until recently for some reason that that all changed.

At the beginning of quarantine, there was a trend where siblings started making TikToks videos together depicting how their relationships got so much closer than before. Every relationship was picture perfect. I saw their relationships and compared them to ours and realized that that wasn't the case for us. We were the exact opposite and went from being super close to not even knowing each other. It wasn't all that bad in the beginning. We would watch movies in the living room together with the whole family until it was time for bed.

I know you are asking what made me change, or what caused this to happen. I really do not know. The world changed and I changed and you changed and everything changed and nothing changed. Every day nothing changes. Every day I lock myself in my room and refuse to leave until I get something to eat from the kitchen. I hear you. I hear the conversations and laughs you share with Saida and Mama and wish I could be there with you guys. And I know sometimes you guys talk about me and ask why I am acting like this and say how you miss the way things used to be. But do you really think I genuinely enjoy being alone in a room not talking to a single person all day long?

I've tried. I've tried overcoming this feeling and tried to be social and make an effort to get out of bed and come to the living room and actually be a family. But I just can't. When I try hanging out with the whole family, I end up getting annoyed and mad over the smallest things and storm out of the room.

One day you yelled at me while crying: "You aren't the sister I loved for all these years. You are a completely different person now. I can't even recognize you anymore." That night I stayed up until 4 in the morning crying silently as you slept in the bed beside me.

But you are right. I'm not the same person I was before quarantine and I don't know why I'm acting like this. I don't feel like myself.

You did not know about any of this and I know you are thinking about what you could've done to prevent me from the pain I'm feeling. But there really is nothing you could do to help because I don't even know what to do to help myself. I stress this so much because I know you feel guilty. There is nothing you did that made me feel this way. I'm just mad. Mad at myself. Mad at you. Mad at the world overall.

You're probably not even going to read this. You won't listen even if you do.

Please....listen.

Sincerely,
Anela

Nineteen

By Melanie Mercado

The first few months of quarantine I was struggling with an eating disorder and dealing with a break-up. I thought it was going to be the relationship that would last a lifetime and I was heartbroken. I felt like my whole world was crashing down and like my chest was caving in, and I couldn't stop the tears. Every day I would eat less and less, until I lost a total of eighteen pounds in less than a month.

Deeper into quarantine, I got a job in an effort to distract myself from everything that had been happening in my personal life. I was kind of trying to put my feelings on hold. That job was very bad for me and my anxiety had never been worse. I ended up getting fired.

When it came to school, I struggled a lot finishing sophomore year, but I struggled the most doing all online classes this year. Teachers are hard to understand, and even though the teachers try, it's hard to stay motivated. My grades have been getting worse.

I lost pieces of myself to others that I doubt I'll ever get back. Maybe those pieces that were taken from me were never meant to stay in the first place. Maybe holding on to an idea of who I was or should be is the worst thing of all. Maybe in losing pieces, like boyfriends, and pounds, and jobs, we find something in ourselves that makes us whole.

Maybe.

Twenty

By Aleyna Koro

The floating rock mentality is a way of thinking about life by way of detachment. Proponents of this narrative say we are all just humans on a floating rock traveling through the vast universe waiting to die. A lot of my friends sometimes see life this way, especially in these times. At one point during these past few months I briefly fell into this mindset as well.

During the first few months of COVID-19, where everyone was isolated, I felt powerfully alone. As time went on and the lockdown extended by more and more weeks, any positive mentality I had at the beginning started to fade. For a few days, I slept on the floor just because I felt this indescribable sadness. That was the first time I have ever thought that maybe life didn't matter. Before that moment, even on my worst days, I always saw life as this mysterious force, and had a desire to live every second of it fully before my time was up. I saw life as an opportunity to discover. However, that night, laying on my bedroom floor, I looked up at the sky through my window and started to wonder what the point of all this pain and hard work was when it only led to death.

I was never fond of the floating rock mentality even before I knew there was a name for it. But that night I understand its attractiveness, and for many nights after would have moments of profound disassociation. I was aware of how I was thinking, and I hated that I felt like this.

As summer approached, I really tried to fix my state of mind. And for the few months of summer I really did. Although I was home for most of the summer and was buried in work, I still felt good. I felt happy even with all that stress. I was able to manage all of it without ever feeling hopeless or unmotivated. However, once the summer ended and once school started it all came crashing down. My "fixed" mentality disappeared. I felt overwhelmed and the smallest, most minor thing would trigger those emotions. One time my mom spilled tea and I cried. When that happened, I was in tears. It was tea. But all those pent-up emotions had to go somewhere. They spilled too.

The whole month of October was full of negative feelings and thoughts. This is where I had the floating rock mentality for the longest time. October felt like the longest and shortest month ever. School was extremely stressful, I found out my old house got sold - that I am finally moving after years of wanting to - and, most saliently, that my parents were finally separating. I was silly to think that all of it would be easier than it actually was. I knew it was going to be difficult. I just didn't know it would be this difficult. I know it could have been worse, but I still wish it was better.

We are all just humans, I thought, floating through space.

Despite the largeness of the universe, I have never felt insignificant even though I am small compared to how big the universe is. I was and still am always passionate about the universe and the planets and the stars and literally everything about outer space. I always wondered how it works the way it does and why. Why is the universe so complex? Why is life so complex? What does it all actually mean? Why does it *matter?*

Life matters. Life may matter differently to different people but, to me, life matters because of this very curiosity. It was the questions themselves that ultimately helped me dismiss the floating rock mentality entirely. It is impossible to just float through the vast universe without any obstacles, without asteroids or meteors. Life, I reckon, is the same.

These "obstacles" during the last few months have affected my life. They are changing me and molding me into a different person, maybe even a better one. Because of these experiences, I have felt my lowest but also have been able to slowly climb back up. I still have these negative thoughts and negative feelings from time to time, but now I try to find ways to make feeling this way easier: Find reasons why life does matter. Question. Attach.

In the end, the planet is just a rock floating through space, a creation through destruction, formed by meteors and asteroids crashing into one another.

Maybe we are too.

Twenty-One

By Leila Abdel-Qader

In March, we had lost school but still retained hope. By November, we lost even that.

I'm blessed that my own life hasn't changed drastically for the worse, like it has for so many. Some people have been forced to close their businesses due to lack of customers. Some have been confined to their households as the risk is too large to go anywhere else. Many have had to fight for their lives. My losses pale in comparison to these. Yet, I have lost one important thing: the anticipation of a hopeful future.

Eight months.

Eight months of social distancing.

Eight months of covering our faces with fabric.

Eight months of worrying about every little thing that we touch outside of our houses.

Eight months of false promises and pipedreams concerning the "end of COVID-19."

Eight months of disinfectant and death.

Currently, rumblings of a second lockdown have come up. It seems as though we are stuck in a continuous cycle: cases rise, the government puts flexible laws in place, and cases lower (which prompt people to believe that the virus is no longer a big deal), and then back to the beginning of higher cases.

Eight months.

How am I meant to believe that things will get better? It's very possible that COVID-19 will become the new normal, perhaps a seasonal event.

The question now isn't when we can have a better future but when we can live in a hopeful present.

Twenty-Two

By Zunairah Rizwan

Ramadan is the ninth month of the Islamic calendar where Muslims show their gratitude for the things they have, practice generosity, and give charity. It is the month where they most embody empathy towards people who are less fortunate through the process of fasting. After a long month of fasting, the time for celebration begins for Muslims with two holidays. As a Muslim, I celebrate Eid twice a year, a time when my families unite to spread happiness and laughter amongst each other. Eid-ul Fitr means the ´festival of the breaking of the fast´ and is celebrated after Ramadan, while Eid-ul Adha means 'feast of the sacrifice´ and is celebrated two months later when many Muslims perform the Hajj, a holy pilgrimage.

Every year on the morning of Eid, my family and I wake up at 6 a.m. with bright smiles across our faces. My sisters and I quickly run to our rooms where we do our makeup and wear the beautiful dresses that we ironed the night before, while my father and brothers rush to the mosque for the Eid prayer. While my father and brother are at the mosque, my sisters and I help our mother make a delicious breakfast so we can all sit together to eat upon their return. Every year as we have breakfast, I can hear my father calling and wishing my family who live in Pakistan *Eid Mubarak* in the distance. The phrase *Eid Mubarak* is a greeting that means "wishing you a blessed Eid" and it is used by Muslims for the holy festivals of Eid al-Fitr and Eid al-Adha.

After wishing tons of people *Eid Mubarak*, my family drives down to South Jersey to spend the day with my grandparents at their house with all my aunts, uncles, and cousins. I love celebrating Eid with my family because all I see around me are children running, uncles giving gifts, aunts working in the kitchen, and huge smiles across my grandparents' faces.

This year, prior to the pandemic, my grandparents had gone to visit Pakistan and got caught overseas without a way to return. Because of the virus and lockdown, their flights kept getting canceled, forcing them to live in Pakistan without their children and grandchildren for 5 months. I was still hopeful that the airports would re-open and they would make it back before my favorite day of the year. However, my hopes were diminished, and they were unable to return. My family could and would not reunite because of COVID. I was utterly distraught, at the family tradition not happening for the first time.

Although Eid-ul- Fitr was not celebrated the way I wished it would be, I was happy that my grandparents were back and would be around when Eid-ul-Adha came around two months later. However, a few weeks before Eid-ul-Adha, my grandmother got admitted to the hospital.

A few days later, she passed away. Because of the pandemic, she was alone for that too. Nobody could wish her a blessed Eid. Nobody could even say goodbye.

Eid-ul Adha is called "the feast of the sacrifice." It is meant to honor Abraham for his willingness to sacrifice his family.

In the Quran, God stops him before he has to.

Twenty-Three

By Shaden Abdelrazeq

"I don't want you all crying the entire time. Cheer up, okay," my mother instructed me. She was standing in the doorway, leaving to take my father to the hospital for the third time since February.

"Okay," I replied, still trembling. "We'll have some ice cream and calm down." We said our goodbyes, and they left. I remember all four of us sisters watching the car from the window and crying. As soon as they were out of sight, my sisters and I all cried some more.

The whole situation was bizarre. We had all been sitting down just minutes earlier, without any worry or fear. Distracted by talking and watching Netflix and YouTube, unaware of what was yet to come. My father was recovering, or at least that is what we thought. Until the doctor called. When he did, I immediately understood that the cycle was not broken, and my father would have to leave home once again.

***

This all started when my father went to the hospital for a stress test in February. I believe it was the nuclear injection they gave him that began killing his immune system. At first, no one had any idea what was wrong. A few days after the stress test he went to see his doctor because he wasn't feeling well and ended up being hospitalized for three weeks. He went in walking but came home in a wheelchair. His body was attacking itself, as if his muscles were viruses. His Creatine Kinase levels were over 19,000. A normal range is between 30 and 300. My father lost tons of weight and could barely walk. He could barely get out of bed without having some of us lift him by his arms. Just as he was getting better, the doctor called once again. He went back to the hospital on his birthday: March 20. He was there for another three weeks. This time, his CK levels were over 36,000. Then he came back home after a few weeks and started his recovery process all over again.

Every time he came back home, he needed therapy to learn how to walk, talk, and even swallow his food. When he first came back, he needed his food to be liquefied, and yet still choked even on that. Over time, he became better, for a little while anyway.

***

Eventually, I graduated, and my family still managed to make the day special, just as my family did with my birthday. They made my fourteenth birthday my Quaranteenth Birthday. It wasn't much: a couple LED lights in my living room. But it meant everything to me. My middle-school graduation party we held outside my house. They got me a cake, some gifts, and had a barbecue. I felt amazing just walking in that gown and taking pictures by the balloons. My father was there for my graduation, though he was inside the house during the barbecue after taking pictures because he needed a specific chair. That didn't matter. He came to see me receive my diploma! And we took pictures. And he reminded me countless times how proud of me he was. That was enough. Over time, my father's recovery process improved. Eventually, he was able to start driving again. This was huge for us, seeing him drive again. We would be so happy that we would go on so many family drives for no reason at all. He would be able to go out again, though he would wear two or three masks for extra protection.

In July, my cousin got engaged! And my dad was there! My father was a different person! He was *dancing*! And he danced the whole night! He danced like never before. He even raised his cane in the air and danced with it like a baton.

***

The rest of July came and went, and August began. Then, around the middle of August, my father went back to the hospital again, for the third time. We all cried. This time, my father's CK levels were over 53,000. We needed to keep his CK levels under control while simultaneously keeping his immune system from attacking his own muscles.

A few days after my father went to the hospital, my mother went back to work after a leave of absence. So now I am left to take care of my sisters. My mother would go to him straight after work, or she would come back home to make us dinner first and then leave again.

One day, we went to surprise my mom and pick her up from visiting my dad. Turns out, she had to stay a little longer than usual because there was something wrong. So we went home, and she came back shortly after. The next day, my sisters and I were at home waiting for my mother to return. I remember just sitting on the couch waiting and wondering what was happening. Ten o'clock rolled around and she still wasn't home.

I called my mom and she said something along the lines of "I'm just waiting for the doctor. We need him to give Baba the medicine." But I worried that wasn't all. I ran to my room and broke down. I was overwhelmed by everything going on: Coronavirus, quarantine, my dad. It was so much.

***

After a week in the hospital, my father returned home. He was doing so much better than all the other times he came back. I hope the cycle ends.

Sometimes, I hear people talk about those with pre-existing conditions on the TV as if they deserve to die because they are weak. Sometimes, I hear them say that hospitals will soon be too full of COVID patients to properly care for those with other illnesses.

I was in eighth grade when this all happened. I am now a freshman in high school.

"I don't want you all crying the entire time," my mother instructs me.

Twenty-Four

By Grace Jerred-Scott

My dad had been wanting to take me and my sister on a night hike for a while, even before the pandemic hit. We all thought walking through the woods at night would be fun and interesting and even thrilling; it would be a new adventure for us all. We finally got the chance to go the night before Halloween: October 30th. My sister was a nervous wreck because the eve of Halloween seemed like the perfect night to be murdered in the dead of night in the middle of the woods. My dad and I just thought that the eve of Halloween would set the mood. In fact, my dad and I were even considering hiking up to a cemetery that we knew of, instead of just going to the lake like we had planned. My sister quickly dismissed that idea and made it very clear that it was not up for discussion either.

We left for the trail at 7:30 p.m., long after the sun had gone down, and we got to the trailhead at 8:30 p.m. It was 30 degrees outside, and we didn't have the sun to warm us. We were cold and shivering the instant we got out of the car. We were bundled up as much as we could have been, and still we were cold. The cold seeped into my bones and chilled me from the inside out. As uncomfortable and almost painful as being that cold was, it was also refreshing. I had gone so long in the temperature-controlled environment of my house that I had forgotten what it felt like to be cold. I hadn't been too cold for seven months, and, as odd as it sounds, I missed being uncomfortable. My fingers were pale and numb, and we hadn't even left the car yet. I couldn't feel anything through my fingertips. I was relying on the uneven ground beneath my feet, and the soft breeze passing over my stinging cheeks to keep me tethered to reality.

My dad, my sister, and I set out for the lake when we had gathered all of our things. The silence and stillness of the woods at night was overwhelming. The noise of the highway faded away the instant we started walking on the trail. There were no birds chirping and the breeze that whistled in my ears when we were at the car stopped at the tree line, the forest was too dense for the breeze to make it to where we were.

Not even the leaves under our feet made a sound as we stepped on them. Everything was silent. There was a fog that I didn't notice before and I wasn't able to see through it. The moon was brighter than I had ever seen it, and the fog reflected all that moonlight, giving everything the fog touched a warm, pale glow. There was no one around for miles, and the farther we walked the more distance we put between us and the rest of the world.

The lake took us by surprise. Usually, in the daylight, we can see it long before we reach its shores, but in the dark and the fog, we could hardly see 10 feet ahead of us, let alone a lake that is a mile away. When we did finally get to the lake, we realized that it wasn't what we were expecting to see. It was the correct lake, but it looked completely different at night. The surrounding mountains rose above the water like an impenetrable barrier that kept the world, and all its problems, far away from us. The lake was completely still. There wasn't a single ripple across the entire surface of the water. The stillness of the lake allowed for a perfect reflection of the mountains, the moon, the clouds, and the fog. The only sound was us: our breathing, our hushed whispers, and our footsteps on the frozen ground. I remember pressing my numb and blue fingers to my cheeks, attempting to warm my face, but my fingers were just as cold as my cheeks and neither my cheeks nor my fingers got any warmer. The darkness and the silence pressed in on me, making me feel small and insignificant.

But that was okay. I didn't want to be important, I just wanted to be there.

The longer we stood there, watching the lake in silence, the lighter I felt. I could physically feel the anxiety and the anger and the fear melting off my shoulders. The silence and the stillness quieted my mind, and for the first time in seven months I finally got some peace. The voices in my head weren't screaming at each other and I could feel time passing normally. It felt like the world was slowing down but I wasn't, and I was finally catching up to everything else after months of being left behind. I could still feel all those emotions that once threatened to break me, but the silence kept them in check, and in the silence, they couldn't overtake me. I felt unimportant and untouchable.

I felt free.

As we made our way back to the car, I let my mind stay at the lake. I didn't want to go back to the suffocating noise, and stress, and fear that those mountains protected me from. But the farther away from the lake I was, the less the mountains could block out.

I tried to hold on to the silent serenity as long as I could, desperately trying to close the gap between the rest of the world and me. I didn't want to ignore everything anymore. Right then, at that moment, I decided I didn't want to be left behind again and, unlike before, I was willing to fight to keep up.

I turned on the news for the first time in months when I got home. I didn't tune it out or turn it off, either. I sat and I watched the news. I absorbed and processed all of the information being thrown at me through the television. I did the same thing almost every day after that. I caught up.

All I've heard for 7 months now is that we are a part of history and that one day our children and grandchildren will ask us to tell them stories of what it was like to live through the COVID-19 pandemic and that this is the time to do something big and important for the world. The thing is, being a part of history is hard. It is lonely and scary and frustrating, and I never wanted it. I never wanted to see the news filled with pictures of people dying in makeshift hospitals. I never wanted to live in constant fear for the lives of my loved ones. I never wanted to be confined to my house for so long that I forgot what it felt like to be cold. I never wanted to crave the embrace of my grandmother, who is also my best friend, like I do now.

But that is what being *a part of history* is like. It hurts. A lot.

Though my name may not be written in the textbooks that my children will study in the future, I was a part of history, and I accept that.

I was still. I was here. I am still here.

This is my story.

Acknowledgement

Special thanks for the completion of this book go to the entire administration at Cliffside Park, including Board of Education President James Shelley, Superintendent Michael Romagnino, Principal Larry Pinto, Vice-Principals John Lombardo and Kenneth Schmitt, and Jonathan Jannucci and Georgette Van Vliet. Each has had a hand in creating a nurturing, judgment-free environment where students can both excel and feel comfortable sharing their vulnerabilities. This book would have been impossible without their support and guidance.

Many thanks to all the teachers at CPHS including Joseph Aponte, Dan Helm, Kenneth Russo, and Robert Venezia. You have all made me a better teacher, and I have missed sharing your laughter and joy in person.

Incredible gratitude is owed to Brandy Luderer and Dave Porfido, who together found an old memoir written by Ben and trusted me with his words. I hope I treated it preciously. He is missed.

Many thanks also go to each of the politicians who have shared these students' stories including: Governor Phil Murphy, Senators Cory Booker and Robert Menendez, Congresspeople Madeleine Dean and Josh Gottheimer and Cliffside Park Mayor Thomas Calabrese. Thanks in particular to Congressman Bill Pascrell and his entire staff, most especially Ian Godfrey, who have been tireless in their advocacy for the students at CPHS. Their support of our most vulnerable and amplification of their voices is a needed balm in a troubled world.

Incredible gratitude to everyone who shared the first edition of the book, particularly John Singh and Scott Huver, both of whom managed to get it covered in major news publications. We will never forget how you championed our stories.

Thank you to everyone at the PTSO for helping sell the first edition. Special thanks to Nancy Loiacono and LeeAnn Papadoupalos. Major thanks as well to Jon Matthias for creating not one but two iconic covers to house our stories.

No book can ever be written without the support we get from loved ones. To everyone who loved our students into being even when they were scared themselves: thank you. To everyone who has ever loved me: thank you more. Special thanks to Neal Adler and Beth Adler-Duthé in this regard.

Additional thanks to Jamie Lombardi for believing that I could be a teacher, for inspiring me to pursue that goal, and for helping me over the years to manifest it. Always.

Finally, to the seventy-five students over two editions who opened their hearts and trusted me to share their hurts and their pains and their dreams with the universe: You are the heroes the world has been waiting for. May being The Class of COVID-19 continue to inspire you, but never define you, and may you all learn to let go of lost people and lost things.

And when you do (and you will) remember your old teacher. Find me and tell me how.

About Cliffside Park

The mission of the Cliffside Park School District is to provide a safe, academically focused environment within our culturally diverse community where all students have the opportunity to achieve the New Jersey Student Learning Standards at all grade levels.

About the Editor

Shawn Adler is a teacher of English and Psychology at Cliffside Park High School. A former professional writer for MTV News, Shawn is the editor of three volumes of student memoirs. Years ago, his mother used to ask him if he would rather be right or happy, then tell him he gave the wrong answer, making him neither. He is still trying to learn that lesson.

Made in the USA
Monee, IL
09 March 2021

62359214R00152